AN INTRODUCTION TO COMPOSITION STUDIES

Edited by
ERIKA LINDEMANN
GARY TATE

New York   Oxford
OXFORD UNIVERSITY PRESS
1991

Oxford University Press

Oxford   New York   Toronto
Delhi   Bombay   Calcutta   Madras   Karachi
Petaling Jaya   Singapore   Hong Kong   Tokyo
Nairobi   Dar es Salaam   Cape Town
Melbourne   Auckland
and associated companies in
Berlin   Ibaden

Library of Congress Cataloging-in-Publication Data
An Introduction to composition studies /
edited by Erika Lindemann and Gary Tate.
p. cm. Includes bibliographical references and index.
ISBN 0-19-506363-5
1. English language—Composition and exercises—Study and teaching.
2. English languages—Rhetoric—Study and teaching.
I. Lindemann, Erika.   II. Tate, Gary.
PE1404.I57 1991   808′.042′07—dc20   90-24046

9 8 7 6 5 4 3 2 1

Printed in the United States of America
on acid-free paper

Preface

This book introduces readers to the relatively new academic discipline called, variously, rhetoric and composition, rhetoric, composition, and composition studies. The nine essays that follow attempt to answer several questions about the field: What is the nature of composition studies? What do people in the discipline concern themselves with? What is the relationship between rhetoric and composition, between theory and practice? What do we know about the recent history of the discipline? What bibliographical resources aid the work of composition specialists? How do they conduct their research? How do they interpret advice about teaching writing, especially when such suggestions conflict with one another? What role do departmental and institutional politics play in shaping the careers of composition specialists? What activities and rewards characterize a life in this profession?

Because the discipline is new, having evolved in the last thirty years, many people are unfamiliar with its assumptions, history, bibliographical resources, methods of research, and professional activities. Others who may know something about composition studies are nevertheless uncertain that it deserves the status of a separate discipline. The following essays address both groups of readers.

Composition studies distinguishes itself from other disciplines, whose focus is invariably on a body of knowledge or a set of texts, by its central concern with an *activity*, the act of writing. The major concern of most composition specialists is teaching writing well. To do this work effectively, they also attempt to answer broader questions about literacy by studying composing from historical, social, psychological, political, and academic perspectives, often borrowing useful concepts and methods from other disciplines. As members of an emerging discipline, composition specialists also encounter problems. They must learn new ways of thinking about their field, wrestle with terminology, develop better methods of teaching and research, create adequate bibliographical and research sources, and build support for their work among people who may be hostile, sympathetic, or indifferent toward it. This book discusses both the contributions composition specialists have made and the problems they have yet to solve in their interdisciplinary, collaborative efforts to understand how people learn to write.

Although this brief introduction to composition studies touches on many important topics, it also leaves out much. For example, none of the essays talks explicitly about how to teach writing, although all deal indirectly with this important concern. Nor do any of the essays discuss such particular subspecialities of the discipline as the study of writing outside schools and colleges or the assessment of writing ability. Our approach to the subject has been selective. However, most of the essays in this volume conclude with a list of Suggested Readings. These titles direct readers who want to learn more about a topic to additional sources.

Some may argue that a book written by one author might have brought a single perspective to bear on the work of composition specialists. We believe, however, that no one person today can speak with authority about the variety and richness that characterize work in composition studies. Consequently, we have asked nine knowledgeable people, all of whom have demonstrated their commitment to the field, to address their assigned topics in their own voices. Their unique perspectives reflect one of the current strengths of this new discipline—the vitality and number of voices speaking to important issues about writing and its teaching. Our authors deserve special thanks for having produced such excellent work at a time when most of them were deeply involved with other projects.

Chapel Hill, N.C.   E. L.
December 1990   G. T.

Contents

An Introduction to Composition Studies

The Nature of Composition Studies

Andrea A. Lunsford

THE OHIO STATE UNIVERSITY

After a particularly difficult passage in *A Rhetoric of Motives*, Kenneth Burke says "Let us try again. A direct hit is not likely here. The best one can do is to try different approaches toward the same center, whenever the opportunity arises" (137). In spite of its militaristic language, I've thought of this passage often as I began work on this essay, for it represents, for me, just the kind of circling around and trying again that Burke's words invoke. The center I am circling around is composition studies, the subject of this book, and over the past several years I've taken several approaches to that center, first in essays co-authored with Janice Lauer ("The Place of Rhetoric and Composition in Doctoral Studies") and Cheryl Glenn ("Rhetorical Theory and the Teaching of Writing") and more recently in my Chair's address to the 1989 CCCC Convention ("Composing Ourselves") and in an essay for MLA's third edition of *Introduction to Scholarship* ("Rhetoric and Composition"). Not until Erika Lindemann and Gary Tate invited me to contribute this essay to their volume, however, did I recognize the "circling around" I've been doing as such. Why, then, continue this circling, this series of approaches to the center, the "nature" of composition studies?

I do so both for compelling personal and professional reasons, because I wish to understand, as contextually as possible, why I do what I do (rather in the manner of the series of essays *Harper's* published by celebrated writers on "Why I live where I live"); where our field comes from, what its typical motives and gestures are; and, perhaps most important, how its present moment might best be described. I wish to begin with the personal, however, as a way of emphasizing that the answers I give to the questions just enumerated necessarily constitute a story, a personal narrative that inevitably grows out of my own experi-

3

ences, and further, that calls into question the essentializing or totalizing implications of "The Nature" of composition studies. Insofar as composition studies has a "nature," it is available to us only in multeity, in a multitude of stories, of different approaches.

Charles Moran closes this volume with one such story, and indeed every essay in this volume might be subtitled "A Life in the Profession." The story of my life in the profession began, it now seems to me, the day I picked up Edward P. J. Corbett's *Classical Rhetoric for the Modern Student,* hot off the presses in 1971. Though I'd been teaching for several years, it was Corbett's book that actually *invited* me into a community, that helped me to begin to imagine what a life in the profession of composition studies might become. So I want to remark the importance of invitations in our lives and to stress the ways in which invitations of a particular kind stand for me as a metonymic representation of the nature of composition studies.

To do so of course is to be local and specific, to point to particular invitations, and simply writing these words calls up two such invitations that help me account for why I do what I do, for what composition studies "is" for me. The first occurred in 1976. I was a graduate student working to help create a viable basic writing program. We needed help, so I screwed up my courage and called Mina Shaughnessy. She was deeply involved in completing *Errors and Expectations* and was, as I later learned, not in good health. I had hoped for a phone interview or, at most, perhaps a meeting with her at a conference. "Oh no," she said, in that rich voice that was itself so inviting, "I'll come to help. I'll do whatever I can." And come she did, giving us two days of her energy and insight, always listening to us and our students, and always inviting us to imagine a field into existence. When we worried that many of our colleagues, particularly those working on traditional literary projects, didn't seem to understand what we were doing, why we were so interested in basic writing, much less why we valued it, Professor Shaughnessy said, "Don't worry about anything but your own work. Make it strong and rigorous—and it will be exciting. Eventually one or two of those others will wonder what all the excitement is about and they'll come around to find out. They'll notice your attitude toward students and how it informs what you do. And slowly but surely your work will make its mark."

The second invitation I've referred to also came when I was a graduate student, at work on my dissertation. For part of that work, I needed to perform some fairly simple statistical maneuvers, but I was woefully unprepared to do so and frustrated by my lack of fluency in this new language. Such was my frustration and sense of being out of it (probably defining characteristics of dissertation writing) that I marched up to Lynn Quitman Troyka at a conference and asked if she would point me to some books or articles that would ease me in to the vocabulary of *t*-tests and chi squares. "Oh," she said, having never before so much as set eyes on me, "why don't we just sit down right here and I'll get you started." Half an hour and three pages of diagrams and notes later, she had explained not only how to conduct the statistical tests I was interested in but also the reasons why I should or should not be using them and how they related to theoretical and pedagogical questions I was asking. In his 1988 Conference on College Composition and Communication Chair's address, David Bartholomae said that he thinks of CCCC as the organization that "has made work in composition possible." I wholeheartedly agree—particularly if we remember the importance of invitations to do that work, invitations like those offered by CCCC members Mina Shaughnessy and Lynn Troyka.

That I remember these two incidents so vividly is, of course, a mark of their importance in the story of my life in the profession. But they signify for me more than part of the *rites de passage* I underwent in joining a particular disciplinary community. First, they are characteristic of a particular time (the mid-1970s) and place (the CCCC community), and, more important, of two extraordinary women. They also, however, suggest what I have taken to be the *inviting* nature of composition studies. As I think of Mina Shaughnessy and Lynn Troyka, I think of how open and welcoming they were, of how carefully they listened to my tentative voice, my only partially articulated questions. I think also of their passionate engagement with writing as a subject of theoretical and practical inquiry and their equally passionate engagement with learners. A discipline with these values at its center was one I very much wanted to join—or to help create.

I do not wish through this emphasis on invitations to dismiss or ignore the very real conflicts within composition studies over methodologies, over pedagogical strategies, over theoretical constructs. These and other areas of conflict, which are explored by many essays in this volume, animate composition studies and account in large measure for the liveliness of its intellectual debate. But these conflicts are so vigorous in my opinion precisely because they are in service of what I take to be fairly widespread commitments in the field, commitments epitomized by the "invitings" described above: to listen to the voices of others; to map the theoretical and practical worlds of writing; to link the scholarly and the pedagogical and the practical at every turn; and to make students and learning the heart of our endeavors.

I'd like to suggest that these characteristics can be read into the history of composition studies, that they account in part not only for why I do what I do but for where this field comes from, for some of the soil in which its roots first took hold and grew. As a field, composition studies is an American phenomenon, growing up in the nineteenth century in parallel with several significant educational moves (see, e.g., Berlin, Miller, Horner). Of all those elements in nineteenth-century America I might conceivably focus on here, three seem particularly important for the purposes of this essay. The first is the establishment of the land-grant universities following The Morrill Act of July 2, 1862, designating public lands "equal to thirty thousand acres for each senator and representative in Congress to which the States are respectively entitled by the apportionment under the census of 1860." The growth of these universities represents an egalitarian turn in American higher education, a move to offer such education to those preparing to join American society through venues other than the bar, the pulpit, or the forum, venues such as agriculture, engineering, and other "mechanic" arts and sciences. The land-grant universities welcomed a much broader spectrum of the American public than had heretofore had access to higher education, and these students were by and large untrained in Latin and Greek—the traditional languages of the Academy. As the vernacular slowly became the language of choice in all universities, instruction in composition emerged as a powerful means of immersing students in the skillful use of English, at least partially in the belief that the "right and proper" use of the English language was requisite to participation in the intellectual and economic life of the republic. As Winifred Horner has demonstrated, this egalitarian turn in America partially reflects the Scottish influence provided by the example of The Mechanics' Institutes and other Scottish systems of providing free or relatively inexpensive education and balanced to some degree the elitist British (and later German) influences on American institutions of higher learning.

The history of composition studies parallels another important nineteenth-century phenomenon, the move from oral instruction (and oral participation in society) to the technologies of writing. Michael Halloran and Greg Clark have demonstrated the ways in which orality functioned in our early colleges, and both Jacques Derrida and Susan Miller have shown how an oral paradigm persisted long after writing became the primary mode of communication. Of course, writing had long been part of every student's educational experience; learners ordinarily copied out entire courses of lectures as dictated by their professors. But technological developments in the nineteenth century served to make writing so instrumental to higher education, so ubiquitous, that it, like the air we breathe, was hardly noticeable.

The telegram (1864), for instance, made publication of newspaper stories and commitment of text to print easier and more timely, while the typewriter (1868), hailed as a modern miracle, led to increased standardization as well as to much easier production of written texts. Other inventions, including the mechanical pencil (1822), efficient metal pen points (1940), fountain pens (1850), and the attached eraser (1858), not to mention the availability of cheap durable paper, constitute material changes in the production of discourse that paralleled and aided the increasing move to writing as the primary technology in colleges. And with that technology came the development of composition studies. While scholars such as Elizabeth Eisenstein have analyzed what Raymond Williams calls the "very complex interaction" between technological inventions and "social needs, purposes, and practices" (*Television: Technology and Cultural Form* 14–15), to date the story of technology and composition studies in nineteenth- and twentieth-century America has not been fully told (though see Elizabeth Larsen's dissertation study, which argues that contemporary composing process theory was not a serious possibility until the mid-nineteenth century). Nevertheless, it seems clear that the more efficient, less expensive, and available materials for writing went hand in hand with the growing importance of writing in the new colleges. And the growing numbers of students entering these colleges (the student population more than doubled in the last decades of the century) put increasing pressure on the schools to teach composition.

As the doors to the academy began to open and technological change continued apace, traditionally marginalized groups increasingly sought access to higher education. The nineteenth century saw particularly strong efforts on the part of African-Americans and women of all backgrounds to enter the academy in larger and larger numbers. In fact, Robert Connors has argued that the move from oral to written discourse is at least partially the result of women's entry into colleges and universities. The connection between silence and "woman's place" is of very long standing in the Western tradition, and it was particularly unseemly for women to speak in public. Writing, Connors argues, was more distanced and hence more acceptable ("Feminization"). Whether or not such a causal connection holds, however, it seems probable that the increasing diversity of the student population was inevitably accompanied by linguistic diversity. If students from widely varying backgrounds were coming to college (whether the colleges wanted them there or not) someone had to offer instruction in the linguistic ways of the academy. This someone was increasingly the teacher of composition.

Thus, while it is certainly possible to trace roots of composition studies as far back as the fifth century B.C., it seems to me more pertinent to see our discipline as growing most directly out of nineteenth-century American soil and to see its focus on contextualized written texts—how they come to be and how they are interpreted—as related to material and technological changes and to the move toward increased democratization of education that occurred between 1820 and 1900, moves that I think served as compelling invitations to the development of composition studies.

Readers will no doubt have noted the ways in which this brief excursion into the origins of the field of composition studies echoes to some extent my personal stories of invitation: conditions in the nineteenth century invited composition studies to emerge just as conditions in the 1970s invited me to join the field, and perhaps just as conditions in the 1990s are inviting you to do so today.

What are these conditions that characterize the present moment in composition and hence help account for the nature of the field? Do these conditions offer strong reasons for remaining in the field as well as for joining it? As we move toward the twenty-first century, I believe we find ourselves at a moment most receptive to composition studies for reasons I will sketch in here, but this moment is not without its challenges and dangers.

One condition that serves as a strong current invitation to composition studies is the growing consensus among most disciplines that our realities and systems of knowing are not reflections or givens that are discovered ready made but rather are themselves composed (or constructed, to use the term of choice), that it is only by actively composing our worlds that we can know them. This view of reality as a series of composed texts and of composing or constructing as the acts of bringing those realities to consciousness is, quite simply, the heart of composition studies. As a field, we traditionally ask questions about texts, readers, writers, and contexts—and about the dynamic relation among them through which multiplicitous meanings or realities are constructed. Thus composition studies views composing not as a series of discrete skills or a package of processes to be practiced but as the very way we constitute and know our worlds. As such, composition studies stands as a discipline of central importance in a post-modern era (Schilb and Harkin).

Such a position leads composition studies to look well beyond its own borders and to challenge divisions between disciplines, between genres, and between media. Thus a scholar of composition may draw on anthropology, linguistics, psychology, philosophy, literary theory, neurobiology, or other disciplines in studying the creation and dissemination of written texts. The blurring of disciplinary boundaries raises a number of difficulties for graduate students and scholars in the field, however. How can any one person master the discourses of multiple fields? How viable and valid is the use of one discipline's methodology transferred to another field? While the challenges of transdisciplinary work loom large (see, e.g., Stanley Fish, who in "Being Interdisciplinary Is So Very Hard to Do," argues that such work is impossible), the questions asked by scholars in composition studies demand a constant pushing against disciplinary barriers, a constant invitation to other fields to add insights and help build satisfactory answers to our questions.

Composition studies also challenges traditional genre boundaries, particularly those between "fiction" and "nonfiction" or "literary" and "nonliterary." Arguing that all written texts demand interpretation and are thus potentially of interest to the scholar of writing, compositionists have long argued for viewing student writing not as other or inferior but as worthy of rigorous study (Emig, Shaughnessy, Bartholomae). And long interest in and careful attention to the essay, particularly to its proliferation in late twentieth-century America, raise questions about and push against the categories that rigidly separate, for example, the short story from the essay. Particularly fruitful aid in establishing new theories of genre may grow out of work conducted collaboratively in composition studies and narrative theory.

Closely related to genres are the media through which they are realized, and here once again composition studies addresses the ways in which divisions between speaking, writing, reading, and listening no longer hold. Most obvious, perhaps, is the effect of television, video, and other electronic media: on television, for example, a president addresses the nation orally but works from a written text that is "read" from a monitor and "read" as well by listeners at home who may be recording, taping, or transcribing. Like the blurring between disciplines and between genres, the blurring between and among the media of communication both characterizes the work of composition studies and offers exciting possibilities for future research.

A third condition characterizing the current moment in composition studies is the move beyond the classroom or the academy to study the use of writing in the home, in the community, and in the workplace, to trace the use of language arts in both private and public spheres. As a field, composition studies seems intent on pressing beyond campus boundaries, breaking down the walls of the ivory tower, bridging the surrounding moat, and establishing conversation in the public square. Of the many works that illustrate this move in composition studies, readers of this essay might best look to Mike Rose's *Lives on the Boundary*, a demonstration of how schooling can be connected to community action, to the work of Shirley Brice Heath, and to essays in *The Right to Literacy* that focus on scenes of language learning outside the academy. One outcome of work on *The Right to Literacy* has been a follow-up conference on "The Responsibilities for Literacy" held in Pittsburgh in September 1990. This conference featured speakers and panelists from the United Auto Workers, U.S. Steel, The National Alliance for Business, Levi Strauss, The United States Department of Education, and numerous local and state literacy programs talking to and with teachers of composition about ways of breaking down the barriers between school, home, community, and workplace.

The conditions I have described as characterizing the present moment in composition studies—a focus on the constructed or composed quality of all experience, of all texts; the pressing against disciplinary, genre, and media boundaries; the move to connect the academy to other forums in the private and public space—are all movements beyond the center, all voyages outward, all inviting, I believe, a broad definition of literacy or literacies as the business composition scholars must be about. At the very nexus of composition studies' terministic screen (Burke, *Language as Symbolic Action*), literacy encompasses highly theoretical concerns over the relationship among thought, language, and action; historical concerns over the organization and development of literacy; and pragmatic concerns over how literate behaviors are nurtured and practiced. The study of literacy, like composition studies itself, constantly moves outward, inevitably shading theory into pedagogy, research into practice, cutting across lines of class, age, race, and gender, reaching out to all. But for these very reasons, the study of literacy and the field of composition studies inevitably raise complex political and ethical questions: how will literacy be defined and measured? Who will have access to full and multiple literacies? Who will be denied? What are the responsibilities *of* literacy? Who among us is responsible *for* literacy?

During the last twenty-five years, scholars in composition studies have created an intellectual space in which to study these questions and their accompanying scenes of literacy and literate behaviors. As I have attempted to argue in this brief essay, I see this space, this "nature" of composition studies, as large and loosely bounded, informed by cross-disciplinary, trans-institutional, multiply mediated, multi-genred, multi-voiced, and radically democratic principles. This space is, I also believe, powerfully inviting, but its invitations carry dangers as well. First is the danger that the field will undertheorize the questions of literacy outlined above by looking for stable or monolithic answers or by accepting quick-fix cures for the literacy woes that surround us. Even more important, we may fail to meet the challenge of our own best gestures, may become theorizers cut off from possibilities for effective public action.

This dual challenge—to theorize our questions about literacy and the complex issues they raise while at the same time extending that theorizing at every turn to the practical spheres of private and public life in a democracy—represents for me the high tension and excitement that animate current composition studies today. In an essay that challenged its readers to accept this tension, to move beyond the academy and "dive in" to the work waiting to be done in composition studies, Mina Shaughnessy issued one of our field's strongest invitations. She called for those interested in literacies, in the dynamic relationships among texts, writers, readers, and contexts to move beyond the safe borders of the campus or traditional classroom, to voyage out to meet new learners and new questions waiting on new intellectual and personal horizons. And that, I believe, is the continuing invitation of composition studies: not to focus centripetally on a static center or to hedge round a sure and certain "nature" of our field, but to press beyond the center toward the margins of literate experience and our ways of knowing and learning from them. The following essays in this volume chart the course such navigations may take. It has been the purpose of this essay to invite you to join in this navigation, the continuing exploration of what it means to be fully literate in this or any other century, what it means—in practical, social, and theoretical terms—to create worlds from words spoken, written, and read.

Acknowledgments

I am indebted to the many friends and colleagues who have helped me think productively about our field, and particularly to Lisa Ede, Cheryl Glenn, Erika Lindemann, and Scott Leonard for their careful reading of and commenting on this essay.

Works Cited

Bartholomae, David. "Freshman English, Composition, and CCCC." *College Composition and Communication* 40 (1989): 38–50.

Berlin, James. *Writing Instruction in Nineteenth-Century American Colleges.* Carbondale: Southern Illinois UP, 1984.

Burke, Kenneth. *Language as Symbolic Action: Essays on Life, Literature, and Method.* Berkeley: U of California P, 1966.

———. *A Rhetoric of Motives.* Berkeley: U of California P, 1969.

Clark, Gregory, and S. Michael Halloran. "Theory and Practice in Nineteenth-Century American Rhetoric." Paper presented at the Penn State Conference on Rhetoric and Composition, July 1989, and at the Seventh Biennial Conference of the International Society for the History of Rhetoric, July 1989.

Connors, Robert J. "The Feminization of Rhetoric." Paper presented at the New Directions in Composition Scholarship Conference, University of New Hampshire, October 10–12, 1986.

———. "The Rise and Fall of the Modes of Discourse." *College Composition and Communication* 32 (1981): 444–55.

Corbett, Edward P. J. *Classical Rhetoric for the Modern Student.* 2nd ed. New York: Oxford UP, 1971.

Derrida, Jacques. *Grammatology.* Trans. Gayatri Chakravorty Spivak. Baltimore: The Johns Hopkins UP, 1974.

Eisenstein, Elizabeth. *The Printing Press as an Agent of Change: Communications and Cultural Transformations in Early Modern Europe.* Cambridge: Cambridge UP, 1979.

Emig, Janet. *The Composing Processes of Twelfth Graders.* Research Report No. 13. Urbana, IL: NCTE, 1971.

Fish, Stanley. "Being Interdisciplinary Is So Very Hard to Do." *Profession 89.* New York: MLA, 1989. 15–22.

Heath, Shirley Brice. *Ways with Words: Language, Life, and Work in Communities and Classrooms.* Cambridge, England: Cambridge UP, 1983.

Horner, Winifred Bryan. "The Roots of Modern Writing Instruction: Eighteenth- and Nineteenth-Century Britain." *Rhetoric Review* 8 (1990): 322–45.

Larsen, Elizabeth. "A History of the Composing Process." Diss. U of Wisconsin at Milwaukee, 1983.

Lauer, Janice M., and Andrea A. Lunsford. "The Place of Rhetoric and Composition in Doctoral Studies." *The Future of Doctoral Studies in English.* Ed. Andrea A. Lunsford, Helene Moglen, and James F. Slevin. New York: MLA, 1989. 106–11.

Lunsford, Andrea A. "Composing Ourselves: Politics, Commitment and the Teaching of Writing." *College Composition and Communication* 40 (1990): 71–82.

————. "The Past—and Future—of Rhetorical Instruction." *Proceedings of the Canadian Society for the History of Rhetoric.* Ed. John S. Martin and Christine M. Sutherland. Calgary: CSHR, 1986. 103–28.

————. "Rhetoric and Composition." *Introduction to Scholarship in Modern Languages and Literatures.* Ed. Joseph Gibaldi. 3rd ed. New York: MLA, 1991.

Lunsford, Andrea A., and Cheryl Glenn. "Rhetorical Theory and the Teaching of Writing." *On Literacy and Its Teaching: Issues in English Education.* Ed. Gail E. Hawisher and Anna O. Soter. Albany: SUNY P, 1990. 174–89.

Lunsford, Andrea A., Helene Moglen, and James F. Slevin, eds. *The Right to Literacy.* New York: MLA, 1990.

Miller, Susan. *Rescuing the Subject: A Critical Introduction to Rhetoric and the Writer.* Carbondale: Southern Illinois UP, 1989.

Moran, Charles. "A Life in the Profession." *An Introduction to Composition Studies.* Ed. Erika Lindemann and Gary Tate. New York: Oxford UP, 1991. 160–82.

Rose, Mike. *Lives on the Boundary: The Struggles and Achievements of America's Underprepared.* New York: The Free Press, 1989.

Schilb, John, and Patricia Harkin, eds. *Contending with Words: Composition and Rhetoric in a Post Modern Age.* New York: MLA, forthcoming.

Shaughnessy, Mina. "Diving In: An Introduction to Basic Writing." *College Composition and Communication* 27 (1976): 234–39.

———. *Errors and Expectations: A Guide for the Teacher of Basic Writing.* New York: Oxford UP, 1977.

United States Congress. The Morrill Act. 1862.

Williams, Raymond. *Television: Technology and Cultural Form.* New York: Schocken, 1975.

On "Rhetoric" and "Composition"

John T. Gage

UNIVERSITY OF OREGON

Describing anything like a stable relationship between rhetoric and composition is virtually impossible, since the terms themselves have a variety of meanings and applications. Anyone who presumes to assert what the relationship *really* is or ought to be is looking for trouble. An attempt to review the meanings of these terms, such as the one I am about to undertake, will not be justified by the possibility of fixing or circumscribing the field of "rhetoric and composition," as it is now popularly known. The best that we can hope for is a better understanding of what that field might entail, if it truly combines two fields, rhetoric *and* composition, related to each other in some meaningful way.

Terministic Screens

Of the two words, *composition* has the more stable contemporary meaning. Roughly, it means *the teaching of writing in school,* as in the phrase "the composition curriculum." However, that meaning must be qualified (and here the trouble starts) by observing that it is rarely used to describe the teaching of so-called creative writing, which is most often seen as a separate enterprise, as in the phrase "the composition and creative writing curricula." Not only does the term *composition* thereby take on the implicit meaning of "non-creative writing," but its definition will have to be smoothed over with additions like *the teaching of expository writing* or *the teaching of nonfiction prose writing.* For those composition teachers who view the process they teach as creative (as most do) or who see it as entailing processes shared by creative writers, such a qualification will not do.

This association of *composition* with a presumably lower order of writing (the school theme) and its subsequent separation from the scope of rhetoric as an intellectual and belles-lettristic tradition may well derive from the influence of Alexander Bain's textbook *English Composition and Rhetoric: A Manual* (1866), in which rhetoric revolves primarily around a theory of figurative language and composition around a theory of paragraph construction, both treated psychologically (see Horner, Mulderig). The association of *composition* with such a limited pedagogy contrasts to today's pedagogical practices, in which a wider range of approaches prevails, even if the product is (loosely) circumscribed by the nonfiction essay. Already we are seeing that a single term, *composition,* in fact stands for different concepts and that those concepts are not necessarily compatible.

Even though the term is equivocal in reference to what kind of writing is taught in composition, there is relative agreement about its reference to teaching. The agreement is by no means universal. It should be noted, for instance, that the phenomenon of teaching writing in school (as a separate discipline), despite its European intellectual traditions, is primarily American. The *Oxford English Dictionary* does not include this meaning, familiar to every American English teacher. So, while European students would be familiar with the idea of writing compositions, they would be generally unfamiliar with the idea of composition as a subject separate from other subjects. The use of the term in nineteenth-century American education is almost exclusively in the sense of a subject to be studied and practiced separately from other subjects. But when Edgar Allan Poe wrote his essay entitled "The Principle of Composition" (1846), the term implied no reference to teaching; it meant composition as the activity of writing. And the kind of composition that it referred to was exclusively what is called creative writing now.

Classical sources for using *composition* in any of these senses are scarce and inconclusive. A rhetorical treatise by Dionysius of Halicarnassus (first century B.C.) is traditionally entitled *De Compositione Verborum,* but *compositione* is the Latinization of σύνθεσις, meaning, among other things, arrangement or order, so the treatise might as well be called *On the Arrangement of Words* (Roberts 8–9). It appears from Butler's translation of Quintilian (first century A.D.) that Book X, chapter 5 of the *Institutio Oratoria* concerns "composition," but Quintilian does not use the verb *compono* there but *scribo,* meaning "to write." Quintilian is addressing the question of how the theoretical knowledge of rhetoric he has discussed in the first nine books can be acquired and he distinguishes writing, reading, and speaking as three possible ways. So what strikes the translator as "composition" is in fact a list of exercises in writing, such as translation, paraphrase, and imitation. There is no equivalent of *composition,* in the general American sense, in classical rhetoric, unless it is *rhetoric* itself, although the prescription of particular written exercises (the *progymnasmata*) is roughly equivalent to one sense, that of practicing exercises in writing.

Compositio was commonly used in Roman rhetoric to refer to one of the stages through which a student or rhetor proceeds in the creation of a text: *inventio, dispositio, dictio, compositio.* In such a schema, according to Aldo Scaglione, *compositio,*

> also called *structura,* is the Greek σύνθεσις, which studies the relationship or, rather, the structural order of the parts of the sentences, hence primarily an aspect of syntax . . . but seen from the rhetorician's particular vantage point, namely one which transcends the grammatical criteria of *recte dicere* to rise to the level of *bene dicere.* (Scaglione 24–26)

The term *composition,* in this case as in Dionysius, refers to only one aspect of rhetorical activity, and not at all to what we think of either as "composing," or "composition."

The various meanings discussed here all fall within one or another of the categories devised by Louise Wetherbee Phelps to encompass the "three levels of subject matter" that form composition as a contemporary discipline. These are:

1. Written language as a discursive practice (composition).
2. Teaching written discourse as a practice.
3. Inquiry into practices of written discourse. (Phelps 70)

Phelps' list suggests that "composition" may identify a discipline detached both from practice and from teaching, an "inquiry into practices. . . ." Indeed, the phrase "composition studies" may be gaining currency to describe the study of the process of writing, usually by means of quasi-scientific, empirical methods or according to cognitive or behavioral models. "Composition," in this sense, may not necessarily be guided by the need to teach composition as an activity. It may be, indeed it has become for some, an end in itself. The degrees of detachment from teaching within the field of "composition" may be measured by looking at the categories invented by Stephen M. North in *The Making of Knowledge in Composition,* where "the researchers" are said to "*make* knowledge" while the "practitioners apply it." While North rejects such a firm distinction ultimately, he invents four sub-categories of "researchers," while lumping all teachers of composition, "Composition's rank and file," together under "practitioners." While viewing the practitioner as one kind of knowledge-maker, he does not view researchers as teachers (North 21, 22, 137).

A preference for calling the field "composition studies" may indicate a desire to escape from the relatively recent corruption of *composition* to mean the rule-bound teaching of a narrow range of imposed forms. Such an approach derives in large part from certain handbook aspects of the rhetorical tradition. Consequently, the new term may also signify a desire to separate *composition* from the longer traditions of rhetoric, especially when those traditions are alleged to have outlived their valid-ity (see, e.g., Knoblauch and Brannon 23–47).

Such instabilities of meaning are nothing compared to the vagaries of *rhetoric* itself, a term used to circumscribe a complex discipline with a long history, encompassing the study of oratory, persuasion, poetry, grammar, philology, logic, invention, style, oral performance, writing, teaching, and discourse in general. I will attempt no complete survey. (For the most comprehensive single-volume history of rhetoric, see Conley.) I will only cite some of the conditions that give rise, and have always given rise, to multiplicity in the meaning of this term.

First there is the question of whether *rhetoric* refers to the art or the artifact—singular or plural. The same word can be used to refer to any or, on some occasions, to all of these at once. No such problem is faced by those who speak, for instance, of *poetics, poetry,* and *poems.* But for those who talk of analogous perspectives on rhetoric, it's *rhetoric, rhetoric,* and *rhetoric.* "What are you studying?" "Rhetoric." "What does it teach you to produce?" "Rhetoric." "What is that you are writing?" "Rhetoric." The word itself will not tell you whether it is to be taken to signify a theory, an activity, a body of works or a particular work.

A further, and related, ambiguity haunting the word is its ability to refer either to an aspect of all discourse or to a kind of discourse. Consider the difference between these two questions:

What is the rhetoric of this poem?

Is this poem a work of rhetoric?

In the first case, rhetoric is assumed to be a function of poems, all of which will exhibit some manifestation of rhetoric. In this sense rhetoric is considered to be a property of discourse, like grammar, that cannot not be present in some form. In the second case, however, rhetoric is assumed to be a genre of discourse: some poems are rhetorical, some are not. Rather than a property of all discourse, rhetoric is taken to be a distinguishing feature of some kinds of discourse. This is not a trivial confusion. It is present in many discussions of rhetoric and its relation to composition or other aspects of a curriculum. It is one reason, for instance, that composition and creative writing have sometimes gone their separate ways: one allegedly teaches rhetoric (as a kind of discourse) while the other teaches discourse of the not-rhetoric kind. The same confusion is present whenever the phrase "the rhetoric of poetry" or "the rhetoric of fiction" strikes a critic (such as W. S. Howell 40–42) as a contradiction in terms. (It does so less these days than it used to, before Wayne Booth and Paul de Man each called their—very different—critical approaches rhetoric.) The same confusion results in much talk at cross purposes between rhetoricians in Speech departments and rhetoricians in English departments. In one recent anthology, *American Rhetoric: Context and Criticism,* the meaning of *rhetoric* is any work of the public address kind, and rhetorical criticism therefore means the criticism of works of public address only, from any perspective (Benson 3, 9). In contrast, in another recent collection, Richard McKeon's *Rhetoric: Essays in Invention and Discovery,* the term *rhetoric* is used to refer to the principles of judgment common to the making of all discourse (McKeon, esp. 56 ff.). This would make rhetorical criticism the criticism of any text but only from a particular perspective. Quite a difference.

Even when *rhetoric* is used to refer to an aspect of any piece of discourse, it may be used to refer to different aspects. If to ask "What is the rhetoric of this poem?" is to imply that any poem will have rhetoric in it, it is not self-evident what the question asks one to look for. For some, this question might elicit an examination of the poem's extrinsic form, for others its logical structure, for others its figures of speech, and for others all of these. In one tradition—the Aristotelian—such a question might focus on any aspect of the thought of the poem that results in its persuasive power; in another tradition—the neo-Aristotelian—it might focus in addition on the structure of the poem as a "made thing"; in yet another tradition—the Ramist—such a question would imply a narrow focus on the poem's use of specific figures of diction and nothing else. In recent history, *rhetoric* is used by Chaim Perelman to include "argumentative techniques" of every kind (*Realm* 7) while it is restricted by Paul de Man to mean "the study of tropes and of figures" to the exclusion of "persuasion" (de Man 125). The ultimate, though hardly useful, concession to this variety of uses is illustrated in Jim W. Corder's statement that

> . . . I believe that *all* analysis of writing is rhetorical. I believe that all discussion of writers and writing is rhetorical. I'm even inclined to believe that idle chitchat about writers is rhetorical. All kinds of analysis are forms of rhetorical analysis. (223)

Yet another source of ambiguity comes from the use of *rhetoric* as a term of disparagement. "We have heard enough rhetoric; let us now put rhetoric aside and reason together." Although it would be nice if this usage were limited to politicians who want to call attention to the "mere rhetoric" of some other person's discourse in order to contrast it with their own alleged honesty and sincerity, the use of *rhetoric* as a pejorative term goes back to its very beginnings and has consistently nagged at rhetoricians like a conscience. The first teachers of rhetoric were held in contempt, for good reasons, by some who believed they taught deception and fraud. Later the pejorative meaning of *rhetoric* shifted from deception to bombast, again for good reasons. The tension between those who would see in any rhetoric a deceptive or self-deceptive motive and those who would rescue the term to describe persuasion as such, whether well or ill intentioned, is a recurring theme in the history of rhetoric. Those who study rhetoric today as an ethically neutral activity, or even as an ethically positive one, are not more "correct" in their usage than those who use the term as a disapproving label. They simply use it differently. And no one studying rhetoric within the academy today is free of embarrassment when occasionally asked by outsiders what they do, since in the public mind *rhetoric* often equates with "damned lies."

Furthermore, the same word also applies, indiscriminantly, to the description of techniques for composing and to the prescription of those same techniques. (As I will discuss later, it is hard to know which meaning comes first, either historically or logically.) If I were to give you a book entitled *The Rhetoric of Pickle Labels,* you could not tell from the title alone whether it was a book analyzing the way in which existing pickle labels entice their readers or a book which purported to tell you how to construct enticing pickle labels. Look under *rhetoric* as a title in *Books in Print* for a hodge-podge of these usages. Nor is this confusion trivial for the purposes of the present ramble, since *rhetoric* used in combination with *composition* might refer to one prescriptive art in relation to another prescriptive art, or one descriptive art in relation to a prescriptive one. Textbook publishers consider any book that teaches writing to be "a rhetoric"—even if the methodology of that book is not rhetorical in any other sense—while anthologies of readings which might be analyzed for their rhetoric are not so designated. Yet another related meaning for *rhetoric* is seen in the title of Erika Lindemann's *A Rhetoric for Writing Teachers* in which the term means a body of knowledge and lore of potential use to composition teachers, even though the term is acknowledged to have "a wide range of meaning" in the book itself (35).

I do not mean to imply that in the face of such diversity of meaning one ought to give up using *rhetoric* or *composition* in favor of other, less polysemous, terms. Any other terms one might choose would be susceptible to the same kind of lexical variance. I do mean to suggest, however, that the mere utterance of these terms together does not suffice to identify their relationship, without one's being able to say which of many possible meanings one is calling up. The least we can do is to try to say what we mean when we talk about rhetoric and composition, rather than to assume that others will understand the phrase at face value (even those purporting to work in the same field). Again, I do not mean that every use of the term must include a justification for what it "really means." I have seen too many potentially fruitful discussions of rhetoric bog down, not in latent ambiguity about the term, but in initial, and fruitless, attempts to define it once and for all. *Rhetoric* is simply one of those terms that will remain essentially contested. But I do think that we ought to be able to give an account of how we elect to use the term.

Category Confusions

If both *rhetoric* and *composition* have a range of possible denotations, some of which are incompatible, then the words used together denote a corresponding variety of relations. I'll summarize some of the meanings in order to get at some of these potential relations. The following list is not meant to be complete. I make it, in fact, only half-seriously.

composition I: The act or practice of composing.

    composition I-A: The act or practice of composing nonfiction prose.

composition II: The theory of composing.

    composition II-A: The theory of composing nonfiction prose.

composition III: The prescriptive teaching of composing.

    composition III-A: The prescriptive teaching of nonfiction prose.

        composition III-A-a: The prescriptive teaching of some limited aspect of nonfiction prose (such as correctness or paragraph structure).

rhetoric I: The (prescriptive) art of composing.

    rhetoric I-A: The art of composing any kind of discourse.

        rhetoric I-A-a: The art of fashioning the sentences of any kind of discourse by means of figurative ornamentation.

        rhetoric I-A-b: The art of thinking up arguments to be used in any piece of discourse.

    rhetoric I-B: The art of composing public, persuasive discourse.

        rhetoric I-B-a: The art of composing argumentation.

rhetoric II: The products of the art of composing.

    rhetoric II-A: All composed discourse.

        rhetoric II-A-a: The style or figures of speech present in all composed discourse.

    rhetoric II-B: All public, persuasive discourse.

        rhetoric II-B-a: All argumentative discourse.

rhetoric III: Any specific piece of discourse.

    rhetoric III-A: Any aspect of that work.

        rhetoric III-A-a: The specific style or figures in that work.

    rhetoric III-B: Any specific work of public, persuasive discourse.

        rhetoric III-B-a: Any specific work of argumentation.

rhetoric IV: Any aspect of discourse.

    rhetoric IV-A: The stylistic aspect of discourse.

    rhetoric IV-B: The argumentative aspect of discourse.

rhetoric V: Deceptive discourse.

And so on.

Given this variety, the phrase *rhetoric and composition* could express a mere redundancy (as in *rhetoric I and composition III*), it could express a kind of non-sequitur (as in *rhetoric III-A-a and composition I*), it could express a contradiction in terms (as in *rhetoric II-A and composition III-A*), or it could express a moral outrage (as in *rhetoric V and composition II*). Many of the combinations, however, will result in nothing more than a null-set, insofar as no one who uses the phrase intends such a combination.

Without any further absurd pretense to schematize meanings and combinations of meanings, certain possibilities are nevertheless salient. The phrase *rhetoric and composition* can be the redundant expression of synonyms; it can express different concepts in relation; it can express concepts that do not belong together; or it can express concepts that cancel each other out.

If the terms are synonymous, for instance, if they both mean the prescriptive teaching of nonfiction prose, then we probably ought to drop one or the other. If the terms purport to relate concepts that do not belong together, for instance, if *composition* means teaching correctness at the expense of invention and if *rhetoric* means the analysis of argumentative validity and effectiveness, then we probably ought to rethink the field to which the phrase is applied. If the terms cancel each other out—for instance, if composition means practicing specific prefabricated forms of expression and rhetoric means inventing forms according to the needs of specific occasions—then we probably ought to decide which of the two we wish to teach or practice and let the other go begging. If, however, the phrase is to relate different concepts in a meaningful and useful way, then we ought to decide which of the various meanings of each term can complement and strengthen the other.

In search of such a preferred relation, perhaps it will help to determine whether the phrase *rhetoric and composition* implies subordinate or coordinate relations. Is rhetoric a subcategory of composition, is composition a subcategory of rhetoric, or is there no hierarchy implicit in their relation? Just what are we looking at when we look at one alleged concept through the spectacles of another?

If rhetoric is a subcategory of composition, certain implications follow. Composition, as the superordinate category, would, I presume, take in all aspects of the art of composing, of which rhetoric would be one. In this sense, *rhetoric* could mean the art of composing a certain kind of discourse, such as, say, persuasive. This has precedence in some historical definitions of rhetoric as "the art of persuasion." The implication is, of course, that much, if not most, discourse is not persuasive. Consider, for instance, one of the long-standing commonplaces of composition manuals, the classification of discourse into modes of narration, description, exposition, argument and persuasion. If rhetoric is the art of persuasion, then the student of composition is presumed to encounter "rhetoric" only after having worked up to it by practicing something else first. The same result occurs when *rhetoric* is taken to signify that part of composition having to do with stylistic embellishment, as was once typically the case in textbooks, such as Blaisdell's *Steps in English: Composition-Rhetoric* (1906) in which Part One consists of discussions of letter writing, word meanings, forms of expression, the essay, etc., and Part Two begins with "A Digest of the Principles of Rhetoric," defined as "the science that deals with the placing together of words in such a way as to express, in the best possible manner, the thoughts and feelings which the writer wishes to express" (327–28), and follows with a list of figures of speech.

These usages are not incorrect, as I have tried to suggest in the preceding section of this essay, but they lead to absurdities. As a student, you can't practice composing (through hundreds of pages of textbook) without also practicing rhetoric, whether the word denotes persuasion or style. Try writing without style, or without persuasion. I can't even imagine it. But linear separations, such as textbooks frequently require, often imply that *composition* and *rhetoric* can each command one's exclusive attention.

If composition is a subcategory of rhetoric less absurd consequences follow. It would imply that rhetoric, as the superordinate category, relates to the theory and practice of composing all kinds of discourse, while composition is restricted, possibly, to the specific teaching of written discourse of certain kinds. We have already seen problems with such a view related to the way in which those kinds of discourse are distinguished from others. E. D. Hirsch adduced a different kind of objection to this relationship:

> Rhetoric, then, is the subject closest to composition, both because the concerns of the two subjects overlap in many places and because they are both practical arts. All the more reason, therefore, to warn against a premature

subsumption of composition under rhetoric. The nearness of the fit makes
the subsumption of composition under rhetoric all the more misleading. A
legal statute may be well or badly written, while remaining indifferent to its
emotive or persuasive effects on readers. The same is true of many instructional manuals and even many technical articles. That does not put these
genres beyond the pale. They are highly important kinds of writing, and it is
highly important that they should be well-written. (143)

What Hirsch illustrates here is that the enlargement of the category
rhetoric, in order to subsume *composition* under it, will give rise,
ironically, to a diminished sense of what *rhetoric* is (as a genre of
writing) so that it won't contain the enlarged sense of what *composition*
is. What a strange outcome. Hirsch wants *composition,* then, to be "not
a part of another subject matter but a branch of practical knowledge in
its own right" (143). Just what that is, as a separate thing from rhetoric,
is never clear.

A Network of Symbolic Actions

Not a subordinate, but a coordinate relation between the terms would
have different implications. I said earlier in this essay that any terms one
might use in the place of *rhetoric* or *composition* would be susceptible
to the same kind of lexical variance that I have been illustrating, and I
will now say why I think this is the case. The terms must be multivariant
and polysemous because the activities and products to which they refer
are related to each other in a complex web of nonlinear interconnections. Let me illustrate what I mean by these "interconnections" and
how some different senses of *rhetoric* and *composition* fall into them.

   Given that what I have tried to illustrate here is a circle of circles, I
could start anywhere in describing it and "get around" to the rest. By
"the rhetoric people use" on the left-hand side of the illustration, I
mean the talk, speech-making, writing, and other acts of discourse that
people actually perform. This is the world of activity that Kenneth
Burke has called "symbolic *action*" as opposed to "non-symbolic *motion.*" He says that "Action, so defined, would involve modes of behavior made possible by the acquiring of a conventional, arbitrary symbol
system" (Burke 809). Notice that the dots I have enclosed in this circle
(to represent any possible feature of this discourse) are randomly ar-

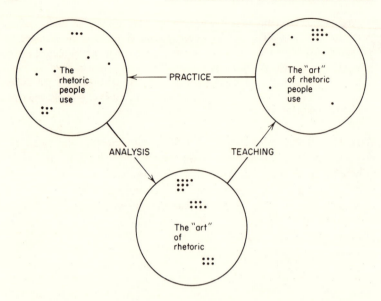

rayed, except for a few that have some kind of "order" to them. This is to signify that whatever is done in this realm is done in ways that are as various as the kinds of real situations, audiences, subjects, discourse conventions, and creative intuitions that might pertain to and constrain symbolic activities, which are multivarious yet derive from some kind of "symbol system," in Burke's sense. Before there was *rhetoric* in the sense of a body of theory *about* using language effectively, there was *rhetoric* in the sense of effectively used language. Homeric speeches give evidence of the existence of *rhetoric* in this sense before the Greeks invented *rhetoric* in the other sense. Yet those speeches also show that "the rhetoric people use" is itself orderly, to a greater or lesser degree, depending on what conventions prevail in the "natural" or unself-conscious production of discourse and under what circumstances. Hence my dots are not entirely random.

Any such language act, or composite of such acts, may become the subject of analysis, the means by which "the rhetoric people use" becomes "the 'art' of rhetoric." Analysis cannot look at everything that occurs in the language act or acts being studied, so it is also a process of selecting from all of the many features of such acts those that are considered by the analyst to be salient and relevant. What conditions this selection is, of course, a matter of what the analyst is attempting to

If there is any commonality at all in the definitions and redefinitions of *rhetoric* that populate the historical tradition, it seems to me to be in the shared assumption of a teleological point of view. Whatever differences prevail, rhetorical descriptions and prescriptions share the principle that the province of rhetoric is what is done in discourse according to the needs of some kind of purpose, end, or intended effect. There are many things one could say about discourse, or inquire into, that no rhetoricians—or anybody else studying discourse as such—has ever bothered with, such as: "How many times does this speech use the letter L?" or "Why is it that my text of Cicero's Verrine orations has chocolate stains on page 97?" or "What is the product of the number of nouns on the left-hand margin multiplied by the number of verbs on the right-hand margin?" or "Why does the word *aluminum* never appear in the Old Testament?" These are questions that have answers. Nothing is stopping anyone from asking and answering them, or millions of others of equal irrelevance. Many questions might legitimately be asked about discourse by sociologists, typesetters, bookbinders, proprietors of bookshops, tax accountants, or recyclers, from their respective interests, that would be of no necessary interest to a rhetorician. Why? Because the rhetorician, despite an equally diverse range of interests in discourse, restricts those interests to aspects of the work that may be assumed to have been under the control of an author for the purpose of attaining some end. Whether the rhetoric in question is the way in which the discourse responds to a situation, the way in which the argument is invented, the way in which the language is constructed, or the way in which the nouns and verbs are proportioned (or any other way), the kind of inquiry that deals with rhetorical features chooses those features for discussion on the assumption that they constitute a *way*. The assumption most basic to a rhetorical point of view, then, is the assumption of authorial control (however *that* is defined) over the possible or available ways in which the discourse might be constructed in order to make a difference. (I do not intend this description to preclude usages such as "social rhetoric," "class rhetoric," or "gender rhetoric," since such phrases will designate, at some level, the productions of authors circumscribed by the society, class, or gender. Indeed, rhetoric in this sense already acknowledges that authorship is a social construct.)

"Make a difference" for whom? In addition to the assumption that the means of discourse are chosen by a writer as a way of attaining some kind of end, rhetoricians tend to assume that that end is situated in the response of an audience, whether it is a desired response or a potential one. Rhetoric, by this analysis, is about the relation of authorially controllable means to the end of potential and possible responses by an audience.

This composite definition is not one that I want to say, again, constitutes what rhetoric *really* means. But few, if any, treatments of rhetoric are without this teleological perspective. If this is the case, *rhetoric* can indeed encompass all of the features of discourse, potentially. But it will encompass them from the point of view of their relation to the whole purpose for which they are adapted. Rhetoric, as a perspective, entails a process of reasoning *down* from wholes to functional parts. Rhetoric sees parts in terms of wholes.

Composition applies to more than just the composition of discourse and in such applications always implies an action of building up, or putting together. The word comes to us as the noun form of the Latin verb *componere,* to put together. In the *OED,* the first meaning listed is "the action of putting together or combining. . . of things as parts or elements of a whole." Thus, it refers as well to the building of a box or a chair out of a specified number and kinds of parts, as it does to the building of an essay (or poem) out of an indefinite number and kind of parts. But parts, as such, constitute the material on which *composing* is performed. *Composition* also potentially encompasses all the features of discourse insofar as they can be built upon and combined with other features. The result is a whole. But the perspective of composition entails a process of reasoning *up* from constituent parts to wholes. Composition sees wholes in term of parts.

Subject to all the vagaries of logomachy I have reviewed in this essay, this difference at least accords implicitly with many of the usages that prevail, and may well provide a way of distinguishing them without imposing unintended meanings on them. If this is not the case, then this distinction at least provides us with a justification for continuing to use the phrase *rhetoric and composition* without reducing either term or without meaning something other than *and.* Both terms by this means keep their largeness. But they keep their difference also. If each perspective, as a mode of reasoning, illuminates the other, then neither will supplant the other. In these senses, any mode of composition will be as good as the rhetoric that justifies it, and any mode of rhetoric will be as good as the composition it enables. This does not solve the inherent problem of ambiguity, of course, but it may rescue the field of rhetoric and composition from the need to solve it.

Suggested Readings

Aristotle. *The "Art" of Rhetoric*. Trans. John Henry Freese. Cambridge, MA: Harvard UP, 1926. See also Grimaldi, William M. A. *Studies in the Philosophy of Aristotle's Rhetoric*. Wiesbaden: Franz Steiner, 1972.

Booth, Wayne C. *Modern Dogma and the Rhetoric of Assent*. Chicago: U of Chicago P, 1974.

Burke, Kenneth. *Counter-Statement*. 2nd ed. Chicago: U of Chicago P, 1957.

Conley, Thomas M. *Rhetoric in the European Tradition*. New York: Longman, 1990.

Connors, Robert J., Lisa Ede, and Andrea Lunsford, eds. *Essays on Classical Rhetoric and Modern Discourse*. Carbondale: Southern Illinois UP, 1984.

Hirsch, E. D., Jr. *The Philosophy of Composition*. Chicago: U of Chicago P, 1977.

Miles, Josephine. *Working Out Ideas: Predication and Other Uses of Language*. Curriculum Projects 5. Berkeley: U of California, Berkeley, Bay Area Writing Project.

North, Stephen M. *The Making of Knowledge in Composition: Portrait of an Emerging Field*. Upper Montclair, NJ: Boynton/Cook, 1987.

Perelman, Chaim. *The Realm of Rhetoric*. Trans. William Kluback. Notre Dame: U of Notre Dame P, 1982.

Plato. *Gorgias* and *Phaedrus*.

Works Cited

Benson, Thomas W., ed. *American Rhetoric: Context and Criticism*. Carbondale: Southern Illinois UP, 1989.

Blaisdell, Thomas C. *Steps in English: Composition-Rhetoric*. New York: American Book Company, 1906.

Burke, Kenneth. "(Nonsymbolic) Motion/(Symbolic) Action." *Critical Inquiry* 4 (Summer 1978): 809–38.

Conley, Thomas M. *Rhetoric in the European Tradition*. New York: Longman, 1990.

Corder, Jim W. "Rhetorical Analysis of Writing." *Teaching Composition: Ten Bibliographical Essays*. Ed. Gary Tate. Fort Worth: Texas Christian UP, 1976. 223–40.

de Man, Paul. "Semiology and Rhetoric." *Textual Strategies: Perspectives in Post-Structuralist Criticism*. Ed. V. Harari Josue. Ithaca: Cornell UP, 1979. 121–40.

Hirsch, E. D., Jr. *The Philosophy of Composition*. Chicago: U of Chicago P, 1977.

Horner, Winifred Bryan. "Writing Instruction in Great Britain: Eighteenth and Nineteenth Centuries." *A Short History of Writing Instruction from Ancient Greece to Twentieth-Century America*. Ed. James J. Murphy. Davis, CA: Hermagoras, 1990. 121–49.

Howell, Wilbur Samuel. *Poetics, Rhetoric, and Logic: Studies in the Basic Disciplines of Criticism*. Ithaca: Cornell UP, 1975.

Knoblauch, C. H., and Lil Brannon. *Rhetorical Traditions and the Teaching of Writing*. Upper Montclair, NJ: Boynton/Cook, 1984.

Lindemann, Erika. *A Rhetoric for Writing Teachers*. 2nd ed. New York: Oxford UP, 1987.

McKeon, Richard. *Rhetoric: Essays in Invention and Discovery*. Ed. Mark Backman. Woodbridge, CT: Ox Bow, 1987.

Mulderig, Gerald P. "Nineteenth-Century Psychology and the Shaping of Alexander Bain's *English Composition and Rhetoric*." *The Rhetorical Tradition and Modern Writing*. Ed. James J. Murphy. New York: MLA, 1982. 95–104.

North, Stephen M. *The Making of Knowledge in Composition: Portrait of an Emerging Field*. Upper Montclair, NJ: Boynton/Cook, 1987.

Perelman, Chaim. *The Realm of Rhetoric*. Trans. William Kluback. Notre Dame: U of Notre Dame P, 1982.

Phelps, Louise Wetherbee. *Composition as a Human Science: Contributions to the Self-Understanding of a Discipline*. New York: Oxford UP, 1988.

Quintilian. *The Institutio Oratoria of Quintilian*. Trans. H. E. Butler. Vol. 4. Cambridge, MA: Harvard UP, 1921.

Roberts, W. Rhys. *Dionysius of Halicarnassus: The Three Literary Letters*. Cambridge, England: The UP, 1901.

Scaglione, Aldo. *The Classical Theory of Composition from Its Origins to the Present: A Historical Survey*. Chapel Hill: U of North Carolina P, 1972.

Theory and Practice

Charles I. Schuster

UNIVERSITY OF WISCONSIN AT MILWAUKEE

Let's begin with what I think is a general assumption in and out of our discipline—one that I favor but which I hope to complicate as I proceed through this essay—namely, that composition studies is essentially defined in terms of practice rather than theory. After all, composition studies is grounded in practice, in the ways that oral and written language are produced, reproduced, learned, taught, shaped, modified— that is, in the variety of practices that anchor rhetoric and composition within our classrooms and our cultures. Students of literature and literary criticism (or most any other discipline, for that matter) may enter into a professional life giving little thought to pedagogy; their interests might center on research or hermeneutics or textual scholarship. They may actually be poor teachers, classroom catastrophes, and not only survive but flourish in their respective departments. In composition studies, so the argument goes, the demands are different. We must first and foremost be teachers. Our disciplinary identities are grounded in practice, in developing writing abilities. When we teach poorly, our ethos is undercut; our authority as specialists in/of writing collapses because we define ourselves and are defined by our colleagues as practitioners. All composition studies specialists are essential Cartesians: we teach; therefore we are.

This identification of composition studies with teaching composition (although teaching is only one form of practice) carries with it considerable ideological freight. Certainly our commitment to the classroom makes us useful to the university community. Composition faculty often have extensive ties with faculty and administrators throughout the university as well as high school English teachers and others in the community interested in promoting literacy. In addition to serving as directors of composition programs and writing centers, we often can be found on teaching improvement councils, campus computer committees, task

33

forces charged with responsibilities for testing and assessment. We work with advisers, registrars, deans, faculty ombudspersons, and academic staff on a wide range of issues and problems: minority recruitment and retention, English as a Second Language policies, learning disabilities—the list is nearly endless. When the administration wants someone to serve in a teaching-centered, practical capacity, faculty in composition studies are often the first to be asked.

Our professional and personal commitment to teaching has other effects. We certainly perceive ourselves as creating knowledge and increased ability among our students, but we also believe that teaching is of great value in our own research and scholarship. After all, teaching is a way of testing the shadowy edges, traveling through unfamiliar territory. Virtually every essay that I have ever written, every project undertaken and completed, for example, can be traced back to the classroom. Whether teaching a first-semester freshman composition course or a graduate seminar, I try to situate that course on the threshold between what I know and what I'd like to discover. To teach is to enter into a series of analyses, investigations, and conversations that lead toward consolidating knowledge, writing, and publishing.

As academics and as advocates of intellectual engagement, most of us possess the desire to maintain our culture and traditions, to invoke ourselves through our students and our written tradition. Through our classrooms and our colloquies, our presentations and published papers, we try to ensure that students and readers will sustain our ideas and values through successive generations. We practice our discipline to insure its survival; we express our normative notions so that they will continue to be invoked. The enabling means by which this is accomplished is modeling, teaching, writing—those activities commonly lumped under the rubric of practice.

In a way unique among disciplines, those of us who participate in composition studies constantly enact our practice. I am referring here to our habits of writing, the rigors and rituals of our composing processes. There is a self-reflexiveness among us, potentially dangerous because it can lead to a strangulating self-consciousness. In practicing what we preach about free writing, drafting, collaborative problem solving, we become aware of ourselves as writers, engage in an unceasing protocol analysis of our own composing strategies. Our pedagogy is thus inescapable: we cannot seal it off from our scholarly enterprise. Even when we are immersed in our most inscrutable intellectual projects, we are teaching ourselves how to teach our students, implicating our pedagogy and our research by our own example. We are both the subject and the object of our disciplinary practice.

It certainly seems to be the case, therefore, that "practice" is a foundational principle of our discipline. We often read ourselves that way in our various discursive practices—that is, in departmental meetings, national conferences, published research, and scholarship. And so are we perceived by most faculty, who conceive of us as bound and embedded in practice in terms of what we teach, what we profess, what we enact as a discipline. Such a reading of composition studies subordinates theory and projects us primarily as an applied discipline. According to this disciplinary definition of ourselves, theory is suspect—and conceivably dangerous—because it often has no direct bearing on our institutional regimen. Theory in some sense subverts; it invites confusion, possibly paralysis. Our discipline is thus identified with undergraduate instruction, with freshman writing, with serving the needs of university and community. The rest of our departmental colleagues may hate it, but we can exult when the English Department is referred to as the "Service" Department, for we subscribe to the fundamental notion of helping students to become better writers, whatever discourse community they claim as theirs. To say that composition studies is founded primarily in the notion of "practice" is, according to this line of argument, virtually to state an oxymoron.

So goes, at least, the argument.

Fifteen years ago, I taught my first rhetoric class. It was indeed a rhetoric class, not a composition class, for it required an emphasis not just on writing, but also on reading, speaking, and listening in supposedly equal parts. This was (and remains) the University of Iowa model, and I am still much in its debt. Given my English major background, I certainly placed more of my emphasis on writing; given the post-1960s atmosphere, I created what I hoped was an exciting and innovative curriculum to stimulate student interest. We read polemical essays by Camus, Malcolm X, Jerry Farber, H. Rap Brown with a special emphasis on student rights and civil rights. We listened to Lenny Bruce, wrote editorials on the ways that print and visual media distorted and subverted that odd quantity known as reality, held in-class debates on grading and the uselessness of college requirements. Given my end-of-semester evaluations and my own perceptions, the students for the most part loved the course.

The problem was that at the end of fifteen weeks they were no better

writers than they were in Week 1, *before* they listened to Simon and
Garfunkel, read about the holocaust, argued through Eldridge Cleaver
and Betty Friedan. My students liked me well enough and enjoyed the
activities I legislated for them. Unfortunately, even though they did a
truckload of essay reading, essay writing, speaking, and listening, none
of the activities produced discernible improvement.

Previous to this stint of teaching rhetoric, I had been one of those
"lucky" teaching assistants who had worked exclusively in the aerie
reaches of the literature curriculum. I had spent three contented years
teaching the sophomore lit survey without worrying about writing. Furthermore, I knew by dint of examination and discussion that my students had indeed improved in their understanding and appreciation of
literary genres. Given my positive experience, I felt positive about
myself as a teacher, and I knew that teaching would make a difference.
So I signed up to teach rhetoric a second semester—now that I had
learned from my mistakes.

Second semester, I taught differently. I used a different reader and a
different writing text. I dropped one thematic focus in favor of another. I
kept my most productive assignments and stole others from my fellow
teaching assistants who claimed that they came with a 100% guaranteed
success rate. That second semester of teaching rhetoric was even more
successful than my first. This time I really knew what I was doing. The
only problem was that at the end of the term, my students wrote no
better than they had during the first week of the term.

Because I failed at teaching writing, I began a graduate concentration
in composition studies.

At the time I thought that I might solve my problem several ways.
First, I could use as a pedagogical model the composition classes I had
taken as a college freshman. Unfortunately I already had. For they had
consisted of reading published essays (in a thick anthology aptly titled
Toward a Liberal Education) and then writing dull essays in response—
or, during the second quarter of instruction, reading literature (*Lord Jim*
is the only text I remember) and then writing dull essays in response. I
can guess what those essays were about, though none has survived:

"Should all students be required to graduate high school?"

"What is a liberal education?"

"Is Lord Jim a hero or a villain?"

"What is a liberal education?"

In my own fashion as a first-time instructor of Rhetoric 101, I had imitated my own education. The texts may have had different titles, but the pedagogy proved identical.

Other alternatives for improving my teaching were also available, most obviously learning some sure-fire teacherly techniques. One of the texts recommended to all new rhetoric instructors was Wilbert J. McKeachie's justly famous *Teaching Tips: A Guidebook for the Beginning College Teacher,* now in its eighth edition. I looked briefly at the book then and have since revisited it. McKeachie is a master of practice: his pedagogical strategies and suggestions take on the patina of 300-year-old English walnut. Revisiting this latest edition, I can still see the book's merits. In his chapter "Organizing Effective Discussions," for example, McKeachie develops a taxonomy based on aims and modes. He offers advice on leading discussions, the use of questions and controversy, buzz groups, inner circles. His advice is invariably practical and always even tempered. "How Can You Have a Discussion if the Students Haven't Read the Assignment?" he asks in a subtitle, and then offers his answer: summarize the material, allow time for students to scan the material, institute quizzes, discuss the problem with the students. Sound advice which I have followed on numerous occasions. And he concludes his chapter by stating quite rightly:

> In general, if the instructor is enthusiastic, friendly, and obviously interested in the subject, students also will be. Let me emphasize again that both lecture and discussion may have advantages at certain points in a course. Skillful teachers will choose the method best adapted to their objectives rather than rigidly sticking to one method only. (43)

What we have here is the promulgation of the golden mean, bent to the aims of pedagogy.

Unfortunately, McKeachie devotes only one chapter to teaching composition, chapter 10. It is entitled: "Term Papers and Teaching Writing" and contains the following subheadings: "Term Papers, Student Reports, Syndicate Methods, The Student Log, Correcting Papers, Giving Feedback, and Teaching Writing." As usual, his advice is judicious and balanced, even Johnsonian in its use of parallelism. He makes useful suggestions about maintaining student logs (or journals) and some fine if limited suggestions about grading and feedback such as "a global grade is more reliable than partial grades, but to help students to learn to write and think, grades are of little value. Students need more information about criteria" (132).

With a bit of effort, I could read through all of McKeachie and learn dozens, hundreds of thoughtful, useful, 5-year/50,000-mile-guaranteed teaching tips. Overall, they all could be summarized generally as follows: Be flexible, Be aware, Be humane, perhaps above all, Be practical. McKeachie is the essence of practice, the best example I know of teaching divorced from theory. His is a *Time/Life* approach to the classroom, a handy guide in this case not to wiring or plumbing but to lecturing and discussing. Like the grammar handbooks we assign so frequently and to so little effect, McKeachie's approach is best used by someone with a good bit of knowledge and considerable motivation. Had I consulted McKeachie extensively and adopted as my own his relentless emphasis on strategy rather than conception, my failure as a teacher would have been assured. I might have developed some dazzling techniques, but they would have served no substantive purpose, or— more dangerous yet—they would have made me a winsome instructor with little or no substance. I would not have been forced to develop that essential habit of tautologic thinking, intellectual self-reflexiveness. *Teaching Tips* is a book I still occasionally recommend, but only to experienced instructors who already possess the habit of thinking about their thinking and now wish further to hone their classroom skills. New instructors fed on a concentrated diet of methodology tend to lose their bearings, or rather, they tend to know where they are but not how they got there or where they are headed.

What I am articulating here is the problem of practice divorced from theory, practice unaware of its own implications. Although I remain sensitive to the claim that composition studies is grounded in practice, that term "practice" needs to be reconceived. Practice in our discipline, for example, should exclude drill, workbook, and other forms of pseudo-composing. It should exclude formulaic responses, be they five-paragraph themes or fifteen-page research essays. It should exclude that whole range of so-called practices that corrode the composition classroom: extensive lecturing about grammar and punctuation, assigning writing as a form of punishment, placing a premium on usage and correctness in the early stages of composing, refusing to engage students in genuine spoken and written conversation, reifying a monolithic (and often linear) composing process to which all students must adhere, creating a pinball-style classroom that careens madly from one clanging thematic focus to another so that no sustained intellectual engagement is possible. Such "practices," destructive to students and teachers, run counter to the major currents within composition studies.

When we associate composition studies with a narrow, anti-theoretical view of practice, we are faced with a major problem: how do we choose among competing practices? As I plan for my first-semester composition course, for example, I compose a potential menu of pedagogical strategies. They include:

Use of journals

Sentence-combining exercises combined with stylistic imitations

Sustained assignment sequence focusing on the theme of "work and play"

Whole-class workshopping of selected student writing

Small-group workshopping of student drafts

Collaborative writing groups, focusing particularly on responding to and revising successive drafts

Daily ten-minute composing on topics generated by the students

A six-week project in which students work through repeated drafts, culminating in an extended essay to be anthologized for the class

Practice in close editing, with examples drawn from their own final essays

Two whole books as required reading (fiction? essays? extended analysis? narrative?)

Additionally, I have to think my way through the kinds of class activities I will foster, my own relation to the students, the kinds of written responses I will make on essays, the criteria I will apply for evaluation, whether I will require a portfolio of written essays, how I will address the various needs—and developmental levels—of my students. On a more global level, I will have to consider overall goals of the course, its relation to other courses in the freshman writing sequence, its institutional purpose—as well as my own purpose in teaching it. The picture gets even more complicated if I am a beginning instructor, relatively powerless, unsure of the implications of my choices, and required to use a departmentally legislated rhetoric textbook and handbook. How am I to survive such teaching, let alone flourish? How am I to make informed choices, particularly when one approach (say sequenced writing assignments) undercuts another (writing groups), when my desire to get my students to invest themselves in their writing seemingly clashes with my obligation to teach them how to survive in the academy? Finally, how do I connect this teaching to my other graduate studies—to the work I am doing in the history of rhetoric, rhetorical theory, literary studies, research methodologies? How do I make of composition studies an integrative discipline that allows me to bring to bear what I am, what I know, what I think?

There is a strong tendency currently among English graduate programs to offer theory as the necessary antidote to practice, as if practice is the problem and theory its solution. That is, if concentration on practice leads to a skills-centered, mechanistic approach to composition studies—to a potential confusion over aims and modes—perhaps immersion in theory will provide a corrective. Certainly, theory is the darling of much post-baccalaureate English. Courses in Deconstruction, Marxism, Feminism, the Prague School, Post-Structuralist Critique, and New Historicism have to a large extent displaced literature courses in the graduate curriculum; at the undergraduate level, the effect is felt all the way to the freshman sequence. It is not unusual now for freshmen enrolled in composition and humanities courses to read selections by Walter Benjamin, Jacques Derrida, Adrienne Rich, Roland Barthes, Helene Cixous. Such an emphasis is understandable: all of us tend to teach what we know, what we find valuable and productive.

The books and journals in composition studies testify to the fundamental importance of theorizing our practice. *College English* devotes entire issues to the post-structuralist debate; in *College Composition and Communication,* we find the leading scholars in our field situating their work within Marxist, Feminist, Derridean, Burkean, Rortian, Althusserian, and Foucaultian contexts. Even our parent organization, the National Council of Teachers of English, long noted for its commitment to curricular issues and K-12 school practice, has recently instituted a "Teacher's Introduction Series" with the publication of Sharon Crowley's excellent *A Teacher's Introduction to Deconstruction.* Worth remembering is that composition studies possesses a substantial theoretical tradition, beginning with Greek thought in the fifth century B.C., which analyzed the power and effect of language, particularly in the domains of the juridical and legislative. The expansive contours of this tradition—its richness, diversity, and heterogeneity—are mapped out in Patricia Bizzell's and Bruce Herzberg's recent collection, *The*

Rhetorical Tradition. Included in this text are the likely figures one would expect to find in such an anthology: Plato, Aristotle, Cicero, George Campbell, Hugh Blair, Richard Whately, Kenneth Burke, Chaim Perelman. What makes the book richer and more invigorating, however, are the less common, more startling inclusions: Gorgias, Boethius, Erasmus, John Locke, Friedrich Nietzsche, Mikhail Bakhtin, Stephen Toulmin, Michel Foucault, Henry Louis Gates, Jr., Helene Cixous, Julia Kristeva. That is, Bizzell and Herzberg are arguing in *The Rhetorical Tradition* that theory in composition studies is multi-disciplinary, catholic in its inclusiveness, concerned with a wide variety of language practices and possibilities.

To read the work of such theorists—and those many others who must necessarily be excluded from any anthology—is essential for anyone concerned with composition studies. The theorists who compose what can be loosely characterized as the rhetorical tradition analyze, describe, explain, and problematize language use in all its varieties, including what we now call the "literary." They attempt to articulate the unfolding implications of that mysterious quantity known as the textual event. As an intellectual enterprise, theory encourages us toward self-reflexiveness. Its universalizing tendency leads us to generalize and synthesize; its abstracting tendency leads us to complicate and even subvert accepted points of view. Theory sets itself against the normative; its thrust is almost always to defamiliarize what we think we know, to compel us to reconsider what we assume that we no longer have to think about.

This is not to say that theory is of universal benefit, or that all theory is useful. Just as there is a variety of competing practices, so is there an extraordinary range of theoretical assumptions and arguments. To read the carefully delineated, taxonomic analyses of Aristotle is much different from reading the elusive, narrative explorations of Plato's dialogues. The search for theory, like the search for practice, entails experimentation and risk. To locate an appropriate theorist is to find someone who possesses similar epistemological assumptions, someone whose analytic method is reasonably congruent with your own.

Moreover theory, at least within composition studies, is inevitably context-bound, concerned as it is with audience, purpose, persuasion, argumentation, aims, affects, and effects. It analyzes language within a matrix of production and dissemination: thus our interests in discourse communities, reader response, Marxism, speech acts. Thus our equivalent concern with administration, freshman composition, the teaching of writing, textbooks, peer tutoring, collaborative learning, high school curricula. Given the contextual nature of our discipline and its emphasis on production and dissemination, it should not be surprising that we find ourselves drawn to an extensive array of disciplines and theorists, from anthropology, psychometrics, and physiology to Clifford Geertz, Jean-Francois Lyotard, and Raymond Williams. For us, these are all rhetorical disciplines and rhetorical theorists to the extent that they examine the production and dissemination of written language within culture. The contextual nature of our discipline in some sense keeps us anchored to the world: like Antaeus, we preserve a certain strength by remaining in touch with the ground, forever conscious of the pull of gravity.

So far, my argument may seem to place "theory" in oppositional tension to "practice," but such a distinction is illusory. The two terms are vexed; they delineate extremist perceptions, caricatures. The opposite of "theory" is not "practice" but rather "thoughtlessness" or even "mindlessness." Theory is not opposed to practice; it is opposed to muddled thought, to confusion. Similarly, the antonym of "practice" is not "theory" but rather laziness, inertia, lack of accomplishment. The "theory/practice" dichotomy is, therefore, a false one. When people argue that "practice" is concrete, specific, tangible and that "theory" is abstract, general, conceptual, they are speaking to an assumed difference that disappears upon closer inspection. The cliché that "theorists think while practitioners do" corresponds to extremist positions that have little bearing on the work most of us accomplish in our professional lives. On the contrary, practice and theory are inseparable, indivisible. Every move made in the classroom is grounded in theory. Every speculative assumption, every theoretical argument no matter how seemingly removed from reading and writing as observed among actual individuals is grounded in practice. Theory and practice thrive in an atmosphere of mutual tension. Clearly each has its extreme proponents, its "pure" practitioners and theorists, but the most exciting and enduring work in composition studies is situated on that tension-filled threshold where theory and practice mutually inform each other.

After all, when I practice the discipline of composition studies, can my teaching be devoid of theory? Or do I also engage in speculative inquiry, both about teaching and about abstract notions such as audience and the interrelational dynamics of language? In the classroom, can I succeed without a sustained theoretical engagement? As a theorist, can I ground my conjectures in anything other than practice? Is my teaching not a form of speculating, and my theorizing not an inherent form of practice? As a specialist and a scholar in composition studies, is it possible for me to separate the practice of what I do from the theory of who I am? As Wayne Booth has made clear, "The distinction between theory and practice becomes problematic; in our profession, to state a theory is to practice our art, to practice it well or ill; it is an invitation to understand, critically" (21). For Booth, this concept of "critical understanding" lies at the heart of our discipline (see Booth 20–26), and it can be achieved only through an amalgamation of theory and practice. Ross Winterowd offers a similar argument in his introduction to *A Teacher's Introduction to Deconstruction* by Sharon Crowley:

> Every English teacher acts on the basis of theory. Unless teaching is a random series of lessons, drills, and readings, chosen willy-nilly, the English class is guided by theories of language, literature, and pedagogy. That is, insofar as teachers choose readings and plan instruction, they are *implementing* a theory. The question, of course, is whether or not teachers understand the theory that guides their instruction. If we do not understand the theoretical context in which we function, we are powerless—unable to rationalize what we do and hence stripped of the ability to argue our case with administrators, boards of education, governments, and special interest groups such as, for example, those advocating and condemning bilingual education. (ix)

The claim I would want to make, then, is that theory is a form of practice and that practice is the operational dimension of theory.

As illustration, I offer excerpts from two radically different texts, texts that on the surface seem to argue for the separation of "practice" from "theory" but which actually support the Booth/Winterowd perspective. The first text is *Through Teachers' Eyes: Portraits of Writing Teachers at Work,* by Sondra Perl and Nancy Wilson; the second an essay by Michel Foucault entitled "What Is an Author?"

In their study of six first- through twelfth-grade writing teachers, Perl and Wilson present a kind of thick description of classroom practice based on observing six different teachers for two years in the Shoreham-Wading River School District in New York. Significantly, *Through Teachers' Eyes* includes no footnotes, no bibliography, few if any scholarly citations or textual allusions. It seemingly ignores the disciplinary conversation and theoretical debates that inform composition studies in favor of a largely narrative and descriptive presentation of teacher activities, classroom progress, and student work. As Perl and Wilson describe their ethnographic approach:

> We take you inside the classroom and show you daily life, not prettied up or made tidy for outsiders but opened up and made visible for other teachers to look at and understand. We show teachers with their doubts and fears, their questions and dilemmas as they try to make writing—its discovery and its power—available to students. In *Through Teachers' Eyes* we show teaching as teachers see it. (xiii)

Although all the teachers presented in the text have the benefit of some intensive National Writing Project pedagogy, they are not all equally successful. *Through Teachers' Eyes* reveals their frustrations and failures as well as their triumphs.

But what looks like transparent reportage and sheer practice is richly laced with theory. Perl and Wilson are aware of the conventions and potential problems of ethnographic research. At the end of her account of the eighth-grade teacher, for example, Perl asks: "Was I too involved? Had I, in ethnographic terms, 'gone native'?" (242). Aware of her sympathy and identification, Perl writes perceptively about her interactive role as both researcher and teacher-colleague. Her understanding of her complicated relationship usefully complicates her research and her conclusions. Perhaps more significantly, Perl and Wilson enter this study with a sophisticated and consciously conceived theory of discourse, one they articulate in their concluding chapter. Here, in a kind of straight-talk for teachers, they advocate their view: the importance of developing writing communities, the necessity for teacher-student reciprocity, the creative use of authority, the willingness of teachers to move from the arbitrary and authoritarian to the provisional, the experimental, the interactive. What seems throughout the book like talk at the level of pure practice actually presumes a wealth of research and theory. Buried in this prose are, to name just a few, the ideas and words of James Moffett, James Britton, the philosophy of the National Writing Project, Lucy Calkins, Donald Graves, numerous texts on cooperative learning and collaboration, and Perl's own work on the composing process. It is this blend of theory and practice that, to reinvoke Booth's phrase, produces critical understanding.

Foucault's "What Is an Author?" might be characterized as pure theory. It is a compact, speculative discussion of authorship in relation to culture and power, a topic of considerable significance to Foucault. My interest here is not to provide a capsule summary of this essay, an impossibility in any case, but to consider just one brief theme expressed by Foucault. Early in his discussion, Foucault considers what is meant by "the idea of the work" (103). He asks:

> What is this curious unity which we designate as a work? Of what elements is it composed? Is it not what an author has written? Difficulties appear immediately. If an individual were not an author, could we say that what he wrote, said, left behind in his papers, of what has been collected of his remarks, could be called a "work"? When Sade was not considered an author, what was the status of his papers? Were they simply rolls of paper onto which he ceaselessly uncoiled his fantasies during his imprisonment? (110)

Foucault's concern in this essay is drawn mainly to authors, to writers with public reputations, to creators of the literary. But what are the implications for all writers, particularly student writers? When I teach freshman writing, I never think of their writerly productions as "work" in the sense that Foucault is explicating. As Joseph Williams makes clear in "The Phenomenology of Error," my assumptions about correctness are to a large extent a function of the writer's authority, indeed the *writing's* authority as a work. What kinds of distorted readings do I give to my students (or, perhaps, to published authors) as a result of this putative notion of "work"? What different kinds of status and interpretation do I assign student writing when it is (a) read and graded as an individual essay produced in class; (b) evaluated anonymously to determine proficiency; (c) considered as part of a research project on composing; (d) viewed in the context of a four-year history of composing in academic settings? How do I view this writing if, ten years later, the writer publishes, becomes famous? What kinds of value do I assign any and all writing by a published author (as opposed to an unpublished author), including notes, fragments, letters, scribblings whether such texts are located on a desk, on a note pad, or within the pages of a manuscript?

What, after all, constitutes a work? And not just what, but when and who and how does such a status get assigned and justified in relation to distributions of power?

For Foucault, the conception of a "work" rests within societal notions of prestige, tradition, author/ity, and power. It also must be understood in the context of other assignments of value in relation to writing: sacral texts, the death of the writer, the absence of the writer, the eternal life of the writer. Foucault is asking us, in effect, what a theory of the work should be—and how such a theory can illuminate what we mean by "an author."

What I am offering here is merely a paper-thin slice of Foucaultian writing, speculations that I am still grappling with as a first-time reader of Foucault's work. My point is that such theorizing—no matter how seemingly complex and abstract—is inseparable from practice. Difficult as Foucault and many other theorists may be to read, their work both rests firmly within the tradition of practice and compels us to successively reconceive it.

The best of recent scholarship in composition studies is similarly not categorizable under the rubric of either theory or practice; neither of those terms suffices. Rather, the scholarly efforts I am characterizing here are positioned on that ambivalent threshold shared by both theory and practice: William Coles' brilliant theoretical narrative of teaching, *The Plural I and After;* Mina Shaughnessy's informed and eloquent account of basic writing, *Errors and Expectations;* Mike Rose's autobiographical *Lives on the Boundary;* and Lev Vygotsky's psycholinguistic exploration of word, meaning, and the growth of mind, *Thought and Language.* These are works that are difficult to categorize; they participate in a number of academic and non-academic genres. This is true of other such works: Janet Emig's personalized and scholarly *The Web of Meaning;* David Bartholomae's and Tony Petrosky's ethnography of basic writing, *Facts, Artifacts, and Counterfacts;* C. H. Knoblauch's and Lil Brannon's iconoclastic and invigorating account of classical and contemporary rhetoric in the classroom, *Rhetorical Traditions and the Teaching of Writing,* or Karen Burke LeFevre's learned and persuasive argument concerning the relations among originality, influence, mind, and language, *Invention as a Social Act.* And I must include two works not commonly considered part of composition studies: Robert Pirsig's novelistic account of rhetorical traveling, *Zen and the Art of Motorcycle Maintenance;* and Mikhail Bakhtin's complex and stylistically sensitive analysis of language, *Problems of Dostoevsky's Poetics.* Such works—and the many others that space does not permit me to list here—provide the basis for the kind of critical understanding that Wayne Booth celebrates.

Writing the History of Our Discipline

Robert J. Connors

UNIVERSITY OF NEW HAMPSHIRE

Composition studies is both the oldest and the newest of the humanities, and our gradual realization of this dual nature is probably the reason for the growing importance of historical study in composition. Traditionally melioristic and oriented toward a beckoning future, composition scholars are realizing that the future can most fruitfully be studied with a knowledge of more than a century's experience in teaching and studying writing. We may not always be able to claim that we see far because we stand on the shoulders of giants; we do, however, stand on the shoulders of thousands of good-willed teachers and writers surprisingly like us, who faced in 1870 or 1930 problems amazingly similar to those we confront each time we enter the classroom. Listening carefully, those of us who have begun to try to hear their voices have found much there we can learn from. Impatient dismissal of the past was a hallmark of our field's early years, and as we mature as a discipline, we will need to draw more and more deeply on the experience of the teachers who came before us. Only in such a context can we discern useful from harmful paths. This essay will be about our development and current state as historians of composition teaching and composition studies.

Rhetorical History and Composition History

We need at the beginning to understand that "history of composition" is not a *sui generis* subfield of composition studies. Like composition studies itself, history of composition is a branch of the larger field of rhetorical studies, which has existed for over 2000 years. Though composition emerged from rhetoric, there is no sense in which we can really

49

say that "rhetoric" ended and "composition" began on any certain date. As James J. Murphy's recent collection *A Short History of Writing Instruction* has shown, instruction in the composition of discourse has always been a part of rhetorical pedagogy. The special field of written rhetoric, which came to be called "composition," grew during the nineteenth century out of the older and more accepted practice and teaching of oral rhetoric, which we can trace in considerable detail all the way back to 500 B.C. The history of composition in rhetorical scholarship has, however, been problematical until recently.

Rhetorical history as a scholarly field has existed for nearly as long as rhetoric itself; rhetoricians have always seemed to feel it important to honor or argue with their forebears. All rhetorical writings contain elements of history, and rhetorical history has thus been remarkably well preserved and documented. Even so, to someone reading the standard modern histories of rhetoric or anthologies of important works, there is a sense of inexplicable hiatus after the eighteenth century. A standard rhetorical history text like Golden, Berquist, and Coleman's *The Rhetoric of Western Thought* gives a good example. In that book, the history of oral discourse begins with Corax and Gorgias in ancient Greece, proceeds through Hellenic and Roman rhetoric and into patristic and medieval works. With the Renaissance we read of a great burst of neoclassical and Ramist activity, all well documented, and then the seventeenth and eighteenth centuries see a tremendous empiricist revolution in rhetoric, culminating between 1776 and 1828 in the ground-breaking works of George Campbell, Hugh Blair, and Richard Whately.

And then, after Whately in 1828, rhetoric as described in these books falls off the edge of the earth. The traditional rhetorical histories end abruptly with Whately, and the rest of the nineteenth century is an echoing tomb. The story picks up again in the 1920s, with I. A. Richards and Kenneth Burke, and from there we hum along merrily through modern to contemporary oral rhetoric, now usually called speech communications. What we see in these books is an intentional excision of a hundred years of rhetorical history, a wiping out of most of the nineteenth century as if it had never existed.

This historical void, which for most of the twentieth century left written rhetoric without a history, is the unfortunate result of the rise of departmentalization in American universities. In early American colleges, oral rhetoric and writing were usually taught by the same generalist professor. There were no academic departments. After the Civil War, however, when scholars began traveling to Germany and bringing back the ideas that would create modern American higher education, the organization of the university into departments of scholars studying similar phenomena seemed natural. Modern English departments appeared quickly, teaching philology, literature, and composition. The older field of oral rhetoric, however, having no Germanic scholarly pedigree, never found a comfortable home in English.[1] In 1914, rhetoric teachers, discouraged by their inferior status in English, left the National Council of Teachers of English to form the National Association of Academic Teachers of Public Speaking, which became the Speech Communication Association—and to form their own separate Departments of Speech. It was in these Speech departments that most of the serious scholarship in rhetorical history has been done in this century.

Speech department scholars defined themselves (naturally, and often polemically) by their interest in oral discourse, and thus we shouldn't be surprised to see a clouding or submergence of the history of written rhetoric in their work. Speech department historians begat histories of an oral rhetoric that seemed to close down or disappear as soon as rhetorical work shifted primarily to written composition in the early nineteenth century. They begin coverage again with the rise of Speech departments as scholarly institutions, creating a new college-based discipline and theory of speech communication. Like literature, composition was seen as an "English concern," and was thus no part of rhetorical history. So high and frowning were departmental walls that it seemed not to matter that most nineteenth-century composition textbooks had "rhetoric" in their titles somewhere, or that their authors clearly saw themselves within the rhetorical tradition. For Speech scholars, rhetoric was oral discourse or it did not exist.

But what of English departments? With composition being taught to great numbers in English, with so many renowned scholars in English from Francis James Child onward, why was no history of composition-rhetoric written? The answer is, sadly, obvious to anyone conversant with the history of English departments.[2] English departments have always been two-tier departments, with the teaching and theorizing about literature given more status and better conditions than the teaching of composition. There was little interest in theorizing about composition or analyzing its history among the burgeoning group of literary scholars, philologists, and critics that controlled English departments after 1895. As the MLA was coalescing and scholars were working to create the organization and bibliographical tools that would result in the modern field of literature, composition teaching increasingly went on in a sort of twilit underground, taught by unwilling graduate student conscripts and badly paid non-tenured instructors. In short, there simply never evolved a discipline of composition studies comparable to literary studies in English. Composition teaching was done, but no degree specialties in composition existed, and no real scholarship surrounded it except for a few articles in education journals and in *College English*. From 1885 until after World War II, composition existed as a practice without a coherent theory or a developed history.

The status of composition did not change until after 1950. The modern field of composition studies grows out of a great change wrought in the American professoriat, especially in English, after World War II. Before that time, college had tended to be for an elite social class and the professors there had been an elect group. After the war, however, the GI Bill made educational loans easy for servicemen to get, and a great rush of veterans into colleges and universities resulted. Colleges groaned at the seams; many grew precipitously to serve all their new students. And from this mass of GI Bill students came a generation of graduate students and young faculty members who changed the face of English. These younger men, who were from all American social classes, brought fresh ideas with them, many of which democratized the staid old English field. In literature they championed A\merican literature and the New Criticism; their teaching changed textual analyses from something only a trained philologist could do to something any earnest student was capable of. In composition their populist influence was even more powerful. Young professors had always been forced to teach composition, and most of them had gritted their teeth, served their time, and escaped to literature as soon as possible. A notable group within this post-World War II generation, however, determined to study composition, analyze it, and try to do it as best it could be done.

At the same time that this GI Bill generation of teachers was beginning to emerge from graduate schools, the general education movement was sweeping America. Based on the idea that too narrow a subject specialization was not useful in life, the General Education movement sought to bring separated disciplines together. In the language arts this General Education movement was called the "communications" movement. The subjects it meant to conflate were reading, writing, speaking, and listening, and the departments that it got talking to one another, after thirty-five years of frigid silence, were Speech and English.

It is here, in the late 1940s and early 1950s, that we can see the emergence of the new field of composition studies, as opposed to composition teaching. The post-World War II generation of active young teachers in English, brought together for the first time with colleagues from the older tradition represented by speech, began to forge during these years a new scholarly field. Its nature was represented by the name they gave the organization they founded in 1949: The Conference on College Composition and Communication. Immediately they established a journal: *College Composition and Communication.* At the beginning of the CCCC's existence, the writing appearing in the journal was nearly always concerned with actual issues in the contemporary teaching of writing. But by the late 1950s, writers on composition issues were beginning to reach out toward collateral fields, looking at the theory behind the practice, beginning to investigate rhetoric and linguistics in a serious way. Composition studies was coming into its own as a discipline. And it was here, in this rapidly changing decade, that the first great research into the history of composition teaching was done: Albert Kitzhaber's 1953 dissertation, *Rhetoric in American Colleges, 1850–1900.*

The Great Exemplar: Albert R. Kitzhaber

Albert Raymond Kitzhaber was born in 1915 and took his MA in 1941. He served in the European Theatre in World War II, returning to work toward his Ph.D. at the University of Washington, and between 1950 and 1953 he researched and wrote his dissertation. *Rhetoric in American Colleges 1850–1900* was written under the direction of Porter G. Perrin, who had himself written a dissertation in 1936 on eighteenth-century American rhetoric. (Perrin, who is now almost forgotten, was one of the great figures of composition teaching in America between 1925 and 1960.) Under Perrin's careful scholarly guidance, Kitzhaber assembled an imposing mass of research materials in nineteenth-century rhetoric and composition, read through and mastered all of it, and then in his writing analyzed and discussed those lost, pivotal fifty years,

1850 to 1900, in a style marked by understated elegance and brilliant synthesis.

Kitzhaber's tone was never one of disinterested scholarship; he looked about him at the serious problems besetting the teaching of writing and sought to trace them to their sources in the theory and practice of post-Civil War rhetoric teachers. "The years from 1850 to 1900 cannot in any sense be called a great period in the history of rhetoric," wrote Kitzhaber. "Composition teaching became, in a very real sense, drudgery of the worst sort, unenlivened by any genuine belief in its value, shackled by an unrealistic theory of writing, and so debased in esteem that men of ability were unwilling to identify themselves with it permanently" (351). He saw his task as providing the necessary information to change the conditions he saw around him: "If a teacher is to have any perspective on his subject, he must know the tradition that lies behind it, know the place of himself and his times in the tradition, and, through this knowledge, be able to put a proper value on new developments in his subject as they appear" (352).

Rhetoric in American Colleges can be coruscating; it is often bitterly critical. With Kitzhaber comes the tendency, seen in much of the later historical work that used his dissertation as a basis, to create heroes and villains out of figures in the history of composition. Kitzhaber's heroes—Fred Newton Scott, Gertrude Buck, John Genung—became the heroes of such second-generation historians as Donald Stewart and James Berlin; his villains—primarily Adams S. Hill and the "Harvard crowd"—became our villains. And for all later historians of composition, Kitzhaber became "the lion in the road": we could not go around him without dealing with his work. That work—its amazing assembly of sources without any previous bibliographic help, its informed analysis of destructive ideas and methods in composition teaching, its attractive division of our forebears into competing camps, and its narrative of the tragic victory of the mechanistic, form-obsessed "bad guys" who created our own troubled period—influenced in ways great and small everything that followed it in composition history.

It's not hyperbolic to state that with Kitzhaber's dissertation the history of composition studies gained its first really respectable work—and then ended for a quarter-century. *Rhetoric in American Colleges 1850–1900* was never published.[3] It remained an underground classic available only from University Microfilms, passed around in *samizdat* Xerox copies by the small group of people interested in composition history.

Kitzhaber went on to a distinguished career at Dartmouth and the University of Oregon, where he continued to work in composition studies and to fight for defensible teaching methods that eschewed both useless traditions and the trendy pedagogical fads of the 1950s and 1960s. And the history of composition in American colleges remained a field little examined. There were, of course, educational histories that touched on composition in college, and a few biographies of figures like Harvard's Barrett Wendell who had also made literary contributions. By and large, however, Kitzhaber's ground-breaking dissertation was not followed up—even by him—during the 1950s and 1960s.

During these years, of course, the general field of composition studies was building itself. Like Whitman's spider, it threw out thread after thread to other disciplines, hoping that some would catch. The primary work during these years was recuperation of the rhetorical tradition, from classical rhetoric onward, and what Janice Lauer calls "analogical-theoretical research," which makes claims for composition studies on the basis of its similarities to other more developed fields, of which the favorites were linguistics and psychology. The technologies of empirical research in composition were re-examined and tuned up, and an improved experimental tradition began. But as the field was creating itself, historical research was a very minor part of it.

The Second Generation of Historical Scholars

Not until composition studies had evolved to the point where it was granting its own specialized doctoral degrees, in the 1970s, do we see the real beginnings of a scholarly tradition in composition history. Before that point, though certain related historical studies had been done in education departments[4] and in speech departments,[5] only Kitzhaber had explored college-level composition history in any detail. Slowly, however, the flowering scholarship turned toward historical issues.

Like such feminist historical work, early composition history was polemical history. Wallace Douglas bitingly reinterpreted Harvard's place in the teaching of writing in his "Rhetoric for the Meritocracy" essay of 1976.[6] Again like feminist scholarship, composition history began to search for marginalized forebears, and the greatest of these, Fred Newton Scott of Michigan, was re-introduced to composition studies by Donald Stewart in a series of articles beginning in 1978. In 1980

James Berlin weighed in with articles in *Freshman English News* and *College English* that helped define the forces that had opposed Fred Scott. Borrowing a term from Richard Young (who had borrowed it from Daniel Fogarty's *Roots for a New Rhetoric*), Berlin called the congeries of teaching methods and theories that had evolved through the nineteenth and early twentieth centuries "current-traditional rhetoric." It was a term of opprobrium, and it stuck.

Beginning with Stewart and Berlin, the scholarly study of the history of composition took off. Slowly at first, then with more speed, scholars began to examine the nineteenth and early twentieth centuries for materials useful to current analytical needs. In 1981 Andrea Lunsford published an essay on rhetoric in nineteenth-century Scots universities, Leo Rockas published an essay on John Genung of Amherst College, and Robert Connors published a piece on the modes of discourse, which won the CCCC's Richard Braddock Award the following year. This organizational imprimatur for historical scholarship seemed to give impetus to a whole new generation of scholars, and from 1983 through the present, historical scholarship in composition has been increasingly accepted as an essential branch of the field.

Most contemporary scholars writing on composition history were trained at the doctoral level in both literature and rhetoric, so a historical perspective and access to historiographic methods are not strange to them. Lunsford, Connors, Katherine Adams, Sharon Crowley, William F. Woods, John Brereton, David Russell, Nan Johnson, David Jolliffe, Anne Ruggles Gere, and others have all applied traditional historical methodologies to the primary and, increasingly, to the secondary sources they use and generate. Like all historians, members of this group bring varied perspectives and intentions to the scholarship they do. Some historical scholars specialize in delineating large movements and trends in composition history, while others tend toward smaller-scale works or straight biography of important figures they have researched. Some prefer an attempt at neutral presentation of their findings, while others are openly polemical, operating from a declared Marxist or vitalist or social-constructionist point of view. In a fairly short period of time, composition history has come to be a microcosm of the larger field of historical scholarship.

Most of the work done thus far in composition history has been in the form of journal articles and book chapters. We seem as yet not to have completed the base-level scholarship necessary to producing in-depth studies of book length. As Donald Stewart put it in 1983, "My best guess is that a truly definitive work on this period cannot be written before 1990."[7] The only longer works done since Kitzhaber have both been by James Berlin: his two monographs *Writing Instruction in Nineteenth-Century American Colleges* in 1984 and *Rhetoric and Reality* in 1987. These books remain the most widely read introductions to composition history used today, and scholars seeking more specific secondary works have to look without much bibliographic assistance through almost every journal in composition studies today; articles on history have appeared in *College English, College Composition and Communication, Freshman English News, Rhetoric Society Quarterly, Rhetoric Review, English Journal, Written Communication, Pre/Text,* and *Rhetorica.* The work done over the past fifteen years has deepened and extended the original territory mapped out by Kitzhaber in 1953, but composition history is still in a very early stage of development. We have a few exemplars, but no masterworks as yet. Small pieces have been admirably accounted for, but the entire picture still remains to be pieced together.

The Question of Sources

Like historians in any field, historians of composition studies face certain practical and methodological problems. Primary among them are problems of sources. Like conscientious practitioners in many historical fields, composition historians at best seek always to work from primary sources. (Though there is a body of secondary sources building up, it is not yet so large or canonical as to be necessary except for background consultation.) And it is in the search for primary sources that the historian most often finds frustration.

Most of our problems with sources are traceable to the marginalized status of composition up until a decade or so ago. When any field of activity is primarily staffed by part-timers and non-tenured teachers with a high turnover rate, we cannot expect many depositories of professional papers to exist. When the primary pedagogical tools and means for training new teachers are "non-scholarly" textbooks, library holdings of them will almost certainly be incomplete. When no Ph.D.s are being granted in a field, we cannot be surprised that the journals for that field are not being stocked by the college library. And when a field is tacitly felt by those controlling the department in which it resides to be either unworthy or actually nonexistent as scholarly activity, we cannot expect that many people will take care to gather together and preserve the physical evidences of it.

Unlike much of previous rhetorical history, written rhetoric is defined by the paper trail it left. But that trail can sometimes be very cold. Certain sources, like the very popular textbooks of the 1890s, are relatively easy to find, while others, such as pedagogical materials and student papers, are quite rare. It is hard, in fact, to imagine any recent historical artifacts more ephemeral than the pedagogical documents that have actually shaped the teaching of writing at specific schools. Syllabi, teachers' notes, correction cards, course descriptions, class exercises, and handouts from the writing courses of the last 100 years do exist, but in minute quantities and only at a few schools. They were simply not saved at most places. Before the advent of easy duplicating technology in the 1940s, copies of typed documents could be made only in limited numbers using the painful and messy carbon paper method, and before typewriting became common in offices around 1900, there was no way of duplicating documents except to set them in type and print them. Thus we have almost no nineteenth-century pedagogical materials that were not printed in some form.

Another important source of information on composition history is, of course, students' papers. Unfortunately, our problem in finding pedagogical ephemera is matched by the problem we have in locating students' papers. Especially in the freshman composition course, it seems, neither students nor their teachers were as likely to keep and save papers as they might be in other, later courses. Except at Harvard, which has extensive archives in both ephemera and papers, no large collection of nineteenth-century composition essays is known currently to exist. There are some isolated papers in college archives here and there, but thus far we have no comprehensive record of what exists and where. So outside of Harvard's courses (which were important models, of course, but not necessarily representative), we have only an impressionistic idea of exactly what student essays were like.

Most of the primary sources accessible to the average historical researcher in composition studies are, then, printed sources of different kinds. Of these, the most often used sources have been textbooks and journals. Since Kitzhaber, who derived the great majority of his information from and based his analyses of rhetorical trends on textbooks, their use as effective reflections of pedagogical reality has been heavy. In an essay in 1982, Susan Miller was the first to critique historians' sometime overuse of texts as sources.[8] Since that time historians have striven to search out as many other kinds of sources as they can. Textbooks remain, however, a major source of information on rhetoric and composition in the nineteenth century and a *sine qua non* for a serious historical investigation. Our histories would be poorer by far without them.

Textbooks are important to any rhetorical historian, but they are of special interest to the composition historian because of their incredible proliferation and variety during the nineteenth century and because, unlike rhetorical treatises of earlier days, textbooks were written and sold with specifically pedagogical intentions.[9] Rhetorical treatises were meant to be read (or heard in lecture form, possibly). Rhetorical textbooks, on the other hand, were meant to be taught in classrooms. We can thus learn a great deal about the rapidly shifting rhetorical theory of the nineteenth century from them (much of that theory never appeared anywhere else) and we can also learn much about how authors thought that theory could be applied and learned through exercises, assignments, authors' introductions, and prefaces. In addition, some of the most fascinating information to be found in old textbooks is no part of the author's intention; student notes, inscriptions, doodles, and *sotto voce* complaints on pages and flyleaves also testify feelingly about how the book was used and its claims received.[10] From Lindley Murray and John Walker in the 1790s through the latest process-oriented rhetoric, textbooks can help the historian get a feel for what rhetorical *ars* and *praxis* both were at any point in American history.

Journals having to do with teaching writing, both those originating in education and those from the field of English, can be very useful to the historian as well. Specialized magazines about education go back surprisingly far into the past (*Barnard's American Journal of Education* started publication in 1856; *New England Journal of Education* started in 1875; *PMLA* began in 1886; *Educational Review* began in 1887; *School Review* started in 1893; and the *English Journal* started in 1912). The great surprise in examining journals and articles even a century old is in noting how "modern" they often sound. Nearly every historian who has looked into these journals, especially the *EJ*, has been astonished by how progressive many of the articles in them seem. But that astonishment should also sound a warning about the unquestioning acceptance of claims made by journal articles. Unlike textbooks, which reflect for better or worse what students were actually supposed to be doing and learning in courses, journal articles often reflect mainly what authors *wished* or *hoped* students were doing or learning.

Indeed, some of the most profound insights that composition historians have come to are based on the disparity between the world of pedagogy set forth in many of the journal articles of the period 1910 to 1940 and what the textbooks show was actually being done in classrooms. Those reading the journals might get a picture of the freshman course across America in the hands of thoughtful, forward-looking teachers who welded experience with humanism and a willingness to seek out and use new methods; even the "discipline in crisis" articles (a century-old genre) give the impression that intelligence and good will shall prevail over the problems. Oral English, or a new grading scale, or using newspapers, or structural grammar, or small-group meetings will make the course pay off. We must examine these articles carefully, however. A few classrooms might have been using small-group meetings and practicing revision as the journals suggested, but thousands of others were sweating through textbook punctuation exercises, or trying to apply Unity, Mass, and Coherence, or attempting to write Three Examples of the Paragraph of Classification. It is only by comparing, year after year, the journals' claims and statements, which were read by a few thousand teachers at most, with the content of textbooks, which were read and used by hundreds of thousands of students, that we begin to get an accurate picture of what composition theory and practice really were like.

Historians must be aware of other sources as well. Professional books about the teaching of writing go back to the 1890s, when the first media-driven "literacy crisis" had produced the freshman composition course as one of its answers. That course created its own methodological problems for curriculum planners, and specialized books for teachers have existed since then. Useful as these books are, they must be examined with the same reservations as journal articles are; they present the world of teaching only as the author sees it, and sometimes as the author hopes it is. Biographies and memoirs of various figures can be very helpful, although few full-scale biographies of central figures in composition history have yet been done and memoirs are about as rare. And only recently has the collection of oral histories from older or retired members of the field begun to be explored.[11] The gathering of these oral histories and recollections is clearly an important task for composition historians, and one we cannot put off.

Locating and evaluating these sources of data have been traditional problems for composition historians. As mentioned, few schools have saved old pedagogical materials or student papers, but I have found library holdings even in the printed sources to be very unpredictable at different universities. Unlike literary historians, composition historians cannot automatically assume that their libraries will have any holdings in their field at all. Old textbooks and even the older professional books have been "de-accessioned" by policy at many libraries. Holdings in the older education journals such as *Barnard's* and the important *Educational Review* are very spotty, and even older volumes of the indispensable *EJ* can be hard to find. Most college libraries get the NCTE journals *College English* and *College Composition and Communication,* but other important journals for historical work—*Freshman English News, Rhetoric Review, Pre/Text, Written Communication, Rhetoric Society Quarterly*—may not be on the shelves. We also face the growing tendency to put older journals on microfilm, which makes the sort of browse-reading so important to historical background tedious and unpleasant.

In addition to confronting problems with primary sources, historians must also cope with inadequate scholarly tools. There are almost none. The field of literary studies has the wonderful MLA Bibliographies as well as a host of more specialized bibliographic tools for both primary and secondary sources. Composition studies, however, has not yet even seriously begun the task of choosing and editing primary sources. Right now, in fact, we do not even have a complete list of such sources; the closest things we have to useful bibliographies of primary texts are the bibliographies at the end of Kitzhaber's and Berlin's books. These lists, while admirable, are far from complete. And scholarly editions of primary sources promise to be long in coming. When it appears in 1991, Andrea Lunsford's edition of Alexander Bain's *English Composition and Rhetoric* of 1866 will be the first scholarly edition of a textbook clearly associated with composition (which is to say, previously ignored by scholarly editors from Speech). For journal articles from the nineteenth and early twentieth centuries, there is no source approaching completeness. General bibliographic sources outside of Donald Stewart's essays for Winifred Horner's two collections, *Historical Rhetoric* in 1980 and *The Present State of Scholarship* in 1983, simply don't exist; each historian has to examine all the primary sources for him- or herself. For secondary work since 1975, of course, the ERIC system is helpful, but it does not cover several important historical journals such as *RSQ* and *Rhetorica*. The *Longman Bibliography* (now the *CCCC Bibliography*), which is issued yearly, bids fair to be our best source on secondary historical work, but it begins only in 1984, and everything before that date must be catch as catch can.

Methodological and Epistemological Issues

For a part of the field that has only been active for a decade or so, composition history has already generated a considerable list of controversies and disputed issues. The disputes tend to fall into methodological and epistemological areas, although most refuse to fit neatly into one class or another.

An example of a dispute that spans categories is the issue of whether composition historians should write histories of theory or histories of practice. One strong tacit tradition in rhetorical history has been to write theoretical histories, narratives that show how one set of ideas was propounded, criticized, adopted, revised. "Influence studies" is the term often given this sort of scholarship in literature. Some of the most impressive works in rhetorical history have been written to trace and categorize these theoretical influences, most notably Wilbur Samuel Howell's two magisterial volumes on English logic and rhetoric from 1500 through 1800, which cover every rhetorical treatise written during those years but make little attempt to situate rhetoric culturally.[12] The other strong tradition has been to describe rhetorical *praxis* and education in the context of their times and cultures, paying more attention to the meaning and uses of the discipline than to the content of its theory. George Kennedy's books on classical rhetoric in Greece and Rome and Brian Vickers' recent *Defense of Rhetoric* exemplify this tradition.

The immense influence of Albert Kitzhaber moved composition history in both directions, but ultimately his work tended to head more toward theoretical than toward cultural histories of composition. Coverage and theoretical analysis of early composition textbooks were Kitzhaber's great strength; like Porter Perrin and Glenn Hess before him, Kitzhaber worked primarily from the artifacts he had gathered and mastered, which were textbooks, and, to a lesser degree, journal articles. Since textbooks remain the largest mine of evidence concerning nineteenth-century composition theory and teaching, and since they remain more easily (although randomly) available to researchers than most other data, and since Kitzhaber had made their use respectable, the early members of the "second generation" of composition historians— primarily Stewart, Berlin, Connors, and Johnson—relied on textbooks to a great extent. As a result, the early work in composition history tends, with the exception of Wallace Douglas' Marxist readings of Harvard records, to be about the theories found in early composition texts and about how those theories evolved.

Even at their most theoretical, however, composition historians have never approached the almost complete lack of interest in culture and practice seen in some theoretical histories of rhetoric. They have remained *involved*. The main reason for this practical and cultural focus in composition history has been the fact that most composition historians are also writing teachers. They are immediately implicated in their subject. Speech historian W. S. Howell could afford a certain distance toward his discovery that Adam Smith in 1749 approached rhetoric with more acumen than John Holmes did in 1755. The fact may have been interesting, but the work of neither of them affected Howell and his daily world of professional reality very much. From Kitzhaber on, however, composition historians have never had the luxury of scholarly distance. They exist, as composition specialists have for a century, in a world of complex social and institutional problems whose solution is writing teachers' charge, and thus even the theoretical and "textbook" histories of the field have always been implicitly polemical. We followed Kitzhaber not only to his sources, but also to the sometimes savage indignation about current conditions that often characterized his work.

So Kitzhaber's methodological legacy has been two-pronged; early composition history had a tendency to look at the past in terms of its theory and textbooks, and it had a distinct tendency to view the past through the sometimes narrow lens of how it seemed to affect the troubled present. We found the works of our heroes—Fred Newton Scott, Gertrude Buck, Joseph Denney, Franz Theremin, Henry Day, C. S. Baldwin, Sterling Leonard, Porter Perrin—and celebrated them. We traced the elements in composition teaching that we thought were questionable back to their lairs in the works of our pantheon of villains and dupes—Samuel Newman, Richard Whately, Alexander Bain, Adam S.

Hill, Barrett Wendell, John Genung, Edwin Woolley, John Warriner, John Hodges. This early work was clearly *sided* history.

The perspective on American composition taken in most of these analyses is easy to understand in retrospect: historians writing in a troubled present constructed a narrative of its genesis based on sources at hand. Thus the metanarrative of most work before 1984 or so might have the subtitle "Decline and Fall." It was a tragic tale of bad theory driving out good, of the loss of the liberal tradition in rhetoric, of calculating, hegemonic Harvard taking over the rhetorical world, of a noble Fred Newton Scott fighting a hopeless rear-guard action against encroaching barbarisms like "grammar" and "workbooks." It ended with the ugly triumph of Bain's formalism over Emerson's and Theremin's idealism and with the onset of our current Iron Age, where until recently the lamp of rhetorical humanism guttered low.

This was a rattling good story, and in certain ways it is even an accurate one. But it was not the complete story, and work in composition history since 1985 has been struggling to add some depth to the all-too-simple tale of Decline and Fall. The essential problems with the old narrative are, first, that it ignores or discounts too much information we now have, and, second, that it does not look deeply enough into the social, cultural, and ideological contexts of rhetoric and composition as they developed in their own eras. For instance, it was a natural and necessary step to trace paragraph theory back to Alexander Bain in 1866 and then to show how his theory is not accurate or useful according to our current knowledge. The harder task confronting historians now is to draw the analysis out in deeper and stronger ways. What led Bain to this theory? How does it relate to changing ideas of English prose style? Why were teachers attracted to it? What do formal theories suggest about pedagogic attitudes?

Perhaps we see the most important sign of maturation in historical research in the crumbling of the simple heroes-and-villains narrative. While no one would deny Fred Scott his eminence, we no longer see his work as the touchstone of all that is True and Good. And after more than thirty years as everyone's *bête noire*, Harvard's A. S. Hill is being seen as the much more complex thinker and actor that he was.[13] We are looking at a broader range of sources and learning that our metanarrative has been too simple. While I would hope that composition history never completely loses touch with the dissatisfaction that fueled its earliest works with fervor and gave meaning and passion to its narratives, our work is richer now. Historians' growing awareness of the causal complexities and sociocultural motivations that are as important as any theoretical history to the development of our field can only make sharper our awareness of current conditions and make more realistic our hopes for solving contemporary problems through understanding them.

Another set of current issues in the writing of composition history has to do with the development of research and with the presentation of data after they've been found. It's our version of the old Platonic/Aristotelian debate about deduction and induction. Some historians tend to see, to research, and to present their findings within overt and carefully created frameworks of meaning, and others eschew this approach. Of contemporary historians, James Berlin is probably the best-known "framework" researcher. In each of his books, Berlin creates a taxonomic structure and follows its implications by fitting various figures and works into it; in *Writing Instruction in Nineteenth-Century American Colleges* his taxonomy breaks nineteenth-century rhetoric into classical, psychological-epistemological, and romantic types, while in *Rhetoric and Reality* he classifies twentieth-century movements into objective, subjective, and transactional classes. Wallace Douglas' Marxist analyses, which use an existing class-structure perspective, are also examples of "framework" research.

Other historians opt for a more inductively derived historical narration, one that takes up a problem at the "beginning"—the first place their research can discover it—and follows it through to contemporary times, or that traces the work and influence of one figure. Paul Rodgers on the Bainian organic paragraph, or David Russell on writing across the curriculum, or my work on the development of handbooks are all examples of problem- or figure-based history.

Both the overt framework histories and the problem- or figure-based works are, of course, subject to the criticism that they present narratives based on *a priori* viewpoints that control and constrain the research beneath them. Berlin chooses his classes, then seeks evidence that reifies them; I start with an *a priori* definition of handbooks and only look at books that fulfill that definition. I cannot think of any work of composition history that cannot to some degree be accused of this sort of *a priori* subjectivism; historians disagree mainly on how much of it exists. In a review of *Writing Instruction in Nineteenth-Century American Colleges*, I once critiqued James Berlin for filtering his research effort through powerful terministic screens and for failing to take important alternate perspectives into consideration. Berlin's reply was that such screens are inevitable in any research project, and that since objectivity is impossible, any historical research project is automatically interpretive and thus radically subjective; all a historian can do is try to be aware of the terministic screens that exist for him or her.

This whole issue of how and when a researcher reaches closure—of where the data she is discovering begin to assemble themselves in her mind into a structure that will form a thesis claim and will then inevitably guide and constrain subsequent research—leads to the great historiographic question of facts versus interpretations. Some of the field's major historians met in an "octolog" at the 1987 CCCC to discuss these complex issues, and in spite of some real methodological disagreements there was surprising agreement from most of the participants. Of the eight panelists discussing "The Politics of Historiography," seven were working historians, and one, Victor Vitanza, was a historiographic theorist. When the dust settled, it was clear that: (1) No one on the panel believed that any "objective" or definitive history was possible or even desirable; all believed that multiple histories are possible and desirable; (2) The seven working historians all believed, tacitly or explicitly, that "evidence" or "data" or "sources" or "historical materials" were essential stuff of their day-to-day researches. Of the eight panelists, only Vitanza valorized language and its infinitely regressive possibilities as the central component of history. ("Is there any evidence for evidence?" he asks.)

That there was so much tacit agreement in a panel specifically convened to air disagreements is less surprising when we consider that the participants were rhetoricians as well as historians. They all expressed an essential rhetorical position: that assent could be based both on inartistic proofs—evidence—and on artistic proofs—the perspective, the method of presentation, the language. The working historians all accepted the concept that evidence must be searched for and weighed, that prejudices must be taken into consideration, and that induction and deduction were both necessary parts of historical research and writing.

The entire question of historiographic theory animating this 1987 octolog has been brought to the fore in the last five years largely through the efforts of Victor Vitanza, who has used his journal *Pre/Text* to advance various radical critiques of current historical works and practices. Vitanza has attracted a brilliant group of younger scholars to the journal, and one of their primary interests has been in historiographic issues. Such scholars as Susan Jarratt, John Schilb, Jan Swearingen, and James Berlin have weighed in with historiographic articles in *Pre/Text*. Although only Schilb (and, to a lesser extent, Jarratt) might be said to hold many ideas in common with Vitanza, the general effect of Vitanza's efforts has been to valorize historiographic questions. Since 1986, the theoretical and epistemological issues surrounding the writing of history have been much discussed.

The proponents of "revisionist historiography," as it has come to be called, fall roughly into two camps: those who seek to promote a specific program or perspective, and those who point out the incompleteness, potential for totalization, or naivete of any specific program or perspective. Into the former camp might fall Sharon Crowley and Jan Swearingen, who have both been engaged in recovering heretofore marginalized figures in rhetorical history: the sophists and women. Here, too, we find James Berlin and Wallace Douglas, who take the perspective of neo-Marxists and argue for dialectical history and class-based historical analyses. The implicit program of this group is action-based; they make the claim that traditional histories are biased, or incomplete, or controlled by sexist or racist or class purposes.

The other group of revisionist historiographers are the epistemological radicals, primarily Victor Vitanza, John Schilb, and Susan Jarratt. (It is interesting to note that with the exception of Jarratt, who is the least radical and most obviously "political" of the group, the epistemological radicals have themselves primarily written critiques of historical writing rather than history itself.) The critiques coming from this end of the table mainly descend from the interpretive issues popularly argued over in literary criticism during the past fifteen years: the undecidability of meaning in texts; the aporias that riddle every text and source; the interplay of social conditioning and understanding or ordering of meaning; the hegemony of linearity and "clearness" as criteria for worth in historical writing; the utter lack of support for any concept of objectivity. In radically undercutting meaning systems, Vitanza is probably the most extreme; like his eidolons Deleuze and Guattari, his own prose style is deliberately playful and hallucinatory, and his suspicion of all proffered meaning-systems as totalizing and potentially fascistic makes him the great epistemological anarchist in the field.

Thus far the working historians have tended to react to the Vitanza position with a mixture of humor, discomfort, and distracted annoyance.[14] We cannot supply proofs for proof, in Vitanza's terms, but thus far no historian has been willing to allow the theoretical uncertainty underlying his or her making of meaning to close down the enterprise. We may argue about the relative power of facts versus interpretations, but finally the community of working historians feels constrained by and dependent on both. All we can do is continue to be aware of the necessary balance between induction and deduction in any research enterprise, trying to avoid totalizing perspectives that force us to closure too early in the research process. No historian sets out deliberately to twist the truth, but Vitanza's critique remains a salutary reminder that our natural prejudices constantly create terministic screens that control what we see—and can control what we look for as researchers.

The writing of the history of composition is still at a very early stage. Much remains to be done. We need to continue looking closely at the connections between rhetoric and writing instruction—indeed, at *all* the issues surrounding the relation of orality and literacy. We need much more work on the period 1790 to 1850, which still remains the subject of only a few articles and dissertations. We still know very little about the teaching and learning of writing outside the United States and Canada; the other English-speaking countries are only beginning to be examined. We need to articulate our knowledge, to connect college issues with the increasingly detailed historical work being done on elementary and secondary schooling. We also must put our research ever more strongly in context by making ourselves aware of the larger issues of class, gender, race, and franchise that have always been the "silent" realities behind college education. The larger issues of literacy and power, which have begun to appear in historical works of the last few years, will be inescapable for historians in the future. Though we may wax nostalgic for the simple days when the Decline and Fall narrative provided continuity, when textbooks clumsily mated and bred without sociocultural influence, and when neat taxonomies made everything understandable, that is not how we think about things anymore.

Historians of composition in the future will need to be both peripatetic and widely read. The primary sources are out there, and finding them—especially the ephemeral pedagogical materials and the almost-as-ephemeral student papers—will be a challenge. We will need to evolve serious collections and depositories of composition materials.[15] In addition to being scholar-gypsies, composition historians of the future will need to immerse themselves in collateral reading about their subjects and periods, as good rhetorical scholars always have. We cannot understand the teaching of writing in 1870 without understanding the causes of the Civil War; we cannot understand the "American English" movement of the 1940s without understanding the McCarthy era. We are ineluctably tied to the movements of our cultures, and as rhetoricians we have to watch the signals. Only then will we write histories truly informed by all the good evidence needed to gain a hearing from an increasingly skeptical discourse community.

Composition history, like rhetorical history, is only one channel of the knowledge we in composition studies must seek. Yet without it, we are cut off from information of vast usefulness. We are not here alone; others have come before us, and from their situations, struggles, victories, and defeats we can build the context that will give our work as teachers and theorists background, substance, and originality. Only by understanding where we came from can we ascertain where we want to go.

Notes

1. For more information on how this lack of scholarly credentials led to the decline of rhetoric, see my essay "The Creation of an Underclass," forthcoming in *The Politics of Writing Instruction.*

2. The classic essay on this question is William Riley Parker's "Where Do English Departments Come From?" *College English* 28 (1967): 339–51.

3. *Rhetoric in American Colleges,* with a new introduction by John Gage, has recently been reprinted (Dallas: Southern Methodist UP, 1991).

4. Glenn Hess' dissertation *An Analysis of Early American Rhetoric and Composition Textbooks from 1784 to 1870* (U of Pittsburgh, 1949), Janet Emig's Qualifying Paper *The Relation of Thought and Language Implicit in Some Early American Rhetoric and Composition Texts* (Harvard, 1963), Gene Piche's *Revision and Reform in the Secondary School English Curriculum 1870–1900* (U of Minnesota, 1967) and Stephen Judy's *The Teaching of English Composition in American Secondary Schools 1850–1893* (Northwestern, 1967) are some of the important examples of work from Education.

5. Warren Guthrie's dissertation *The Development of Rhetorical Theory in America 1635–1850* (Northwestern, 1940) is the only example I know of a historical dissertation from Speech that was not overwhelmingly concerned with oral-discourse issues.

6. This essay is found in Richard Ohmann's *English in America* (New York: Oxford UP, 1976), 97–132.

7. Donald Stewart, "The Nineteenth Century," in *The Present State of Scholarship in Historical and Contemporary Rhetoric* (Columbia: U of Missouri P, 1983), p. 158. From the perspective of 1990, when this was being written, Stewart's assessment looks optimistic.

8. Miller made her charges in her essay "Is There a Text in This Class?" in *Freshman English News* 11 (1982): 22–33.

9. For more information, see my essay "Textbooks and the Evolution of the Discipline," *College Composition and Communication* 37 (May 1986): 178–94.

10. I have before me two books that illustrate this kind of information. In an 1893 copy of Genung's *Rhetorical Analysis,* Nettie Lawson of Bradford Academy has painstakingly written out on the flyleaf four paragraph rules, which she no doubt was asked to consult again and again. Every chapter in the book has pencilled notes from the teacher's lectures. On the other hand, in a 1901 copy of Lockwood and Emerson's *Composition and Rhetoric for Higher Schools,* "Marion, Lily, and Laurena, Members of the Spectator Club" have written "Sing me a song of the south, a song of the sunny south," "On A Beautiful Night With A Beautiful Girl," and the complete lyrics to "When I Get You Alone Tonight." In their own ways, these inscriptions tell the story of an English class, too.

11. There are as yet few examples of these sorts of retrospective interviews. Dixie Goswami and Maureen Butler interviewed Janet Emig in 1983, and parts of those interviews are used in Emig's collection *The Web of Meaning.* Lisa Ede and Andrea Lunsford interviewed Edward P. J. Corbett in 1987, and portions of that interview are used in the *Selected Essays of Edward P. J. Corbett.* R. Gerald Nelms of Ohio State is currently completing a dissertation based on oral histories, but thus far few scholars have ventured out into the field with tape recorder in hand. It must be done, and soon.

12. Wilbur Samuel Howell, *Logic and Rhetoric in England, 1500–1700* (Princeton: Princeton UP, 1956) and *Eighteenth-Century British Logic and Rhetoric* (Princeton: Princeton UP, 1971).

13. See, for instance, David Jolliffe's essay "The Moral Subject in College Composition: A Conceptual Framework and the Case of Harvard, 1865–1900," in *College English* 51 (1989): 163–73. Thomas Newkirk is also doing fascinating research in the Harvard Archives that is showing Harvard's early pedagogy to be strikingly similar to modern "process" and "whole language" pedagogies. Newkirk began to report on this material at CCCC in 1990 with his talk "Barrett Wendell and the Birth of Freshman Composition."

14. The reaction of working historians to the Vitanza position, in fact, is reminiscent of the reactions of Anglo-American literary critics to the early sallies of deconstruction, circa 1975–1982, a mixture of "Very interesting . . ." with "Oh, come *on!*" This position of "glum common sense," as it has been called, will probably have to be maintained until professional necessity

rises and twitches its mantle blue, declaring the Vitanza position to be, as it has declared deconstruction to be, not wrong but merely passé.

15. As of this writing, only one such public collection exists: the Richard S. Beal Collection at the University of New Hampshire.

Suggested Readings

Berlin, James. *Rhetoric and Reality: Writing Instruction in American Colleges, 1900–1985.* Carbondale: Southern Illinois UP, 1987.

————. *Writing Instruction in Nineteenth-Century American Colleges.* Carbondale: Southern Illinois UP, 1984.

Brereton, John, ed. *Traditions of Inquiry.* New York: Oxford UP, 1985.

"Historiography and the Histories of Rhetorics: Revisionary Histories." *PrelText* 8 (Spring/Summer 1987).

Horner, Winifred, ed. *Historical Rhetoric: An Annotated Bibliography of Selected Sources in English.* Boston: G. K. Hall, 1980.

————. *The Present State of Scholarship in Historical and Contemporary Rhetoric.* Rev. ed. Columbia: U of Missouri P, 1990.

Kitzhaber, Albert R. *Rhetoric in American Colleges, 1850–1900.* Dallas: Southern Methodist UP, 1990.

Murphy, James J., ed. *The Rhetorical Tradition and Modern Writing.* New York: MLA, 1982.

————. *A Short History of Writing Instruction from Ancient Greece to Twentieth-Century America.* Davis, CA: Hermagoras, 1990.

"Octalog: The Politics of Historiography." *Rhetoric Review* 7 (Fall 1988): 5–57.

Bibliographical Resources and Problems

Patrick Scott

UNIVERSITY OF SOUTH CAROLINA AT COLUMBIA

There are two good reasons for compositionists now to look carefully at the bibliographical resources in the discipline. First, the resources have changed, and improved, a great deal in the past few years[1] On a practical level, the enormous growth in research and commentary on composition is quite unmanageable if we are unfamiliar with these improved resources. But, second, the problems that composition bibliographers have faced, and the ways they have faced them, tell us a lot about the knowledge-structure (and social structure) of the discipline. By viewing composition through the speculum of its bibliographical structures, we see more sharply how the emergence of modern composition studies has precipitated new configurations of people, purposes, and disciplinary traditions; indeed, its very bibliographical intractability is one of our best clues to the special character of composition's goals and perspectives.

The Background and Prototypes
of Composition Bibliography

At first sight, composition and bibliography would seem culturally antithetical. Compositionists typically have stressed the role of discourse in sharing or shaping or creating a world, while bibliographers have typically seen themselves as value-free technicians, who through impersonal labor enable other researchers to locate all the particles of a preexistent knowledge.

Indeed, for many years, bibliography in composition was simply a non-problem, because few people (at least in English departments)

saw composition as a research field. For English-based compositionists, the teaching of writing was largely a matter of oral folklore,
while the commonest kinds of writing on the topic were the textbook
or the hortatory conference paper directed at fellow-teachers; it seemed
much less important to relate to previous published material than to the
audience's classroom experience.[2]

This practical concern with composition's audience and mission influenced the kind of bibliographical resources that composition scholars
would develop in the 1960s and 1970s. By contrast with bibliographers
in, say, literary history, who aimed to serve subsequent specialist researchers, composition bibliographers have more usually aspired to be
the expert mediator, selecting and synthesizing the results of research
for readers who are practicing teachers or newcomers to the field.
Interestingly, Kuhn made it one of the marks of a new research paradigm
that publication in a field would have this concern with consolidation
and dissemination, rather than just communicating to other specialists.[3]
For good as well as ill, the characteristic genre of composition bibliography was set very early, not as a reference listing, but as the discursive review-essay.

The pattern was established by the founding document of modern
composition studies, the 1963 NCTE report, *Research in Written Composition,* by Richard Braddock, Richard Lloyd-Jones, and Lowell
Schoer.[4] The purpose of the report (which runs to a little over a hundred
pages of text) is to summarize for English teachers the conclusions
reached by experimental and empirical researchers (most based in education departments), and though the report is now nearly thirty years old
it is still a valuable orientation to that research tradition. The final
twenty-five pages are a straight small-print (and unannotated) listing of
research items, now of course long outdated, but what gave the report
its character and impact was the text, with its polemic assertion that
composition should be a knowledge-based field and with its user-friendly summaries of what recent research had concluded (most famously,
about the neutral or negative effects on writing of direct grammar instruction). No bibliographical list alone would ever have had the impact
of this report or reached the same kinds of readership.

Some ten years later, the same review-essay pattern was used for a
second equally influential publication, *Teaching Composition: 10 Bibliographical Essays,* edited by Gary Tate (Fort Worth: Texas Christian
UP, 1976). Tate's contributors included many of those then most influ-

ential in the field, and each essay provided summaries and generous quotation from the composition scholarship being reviewed. In an interesting shift from the 1963 report, the emphasis was no longer on the results of experimental research but on the explication of current ideas and approaches ("theory"); the volume's deserved success was in part because it provided a wide-ranging and readable introduction to what active compositionists had been talking about. The topics were broad-based issues of theory or pedagogy ("Invention," "Basic Writing," "Approaches to the Study of Style"), and the shared humanistic values and pedagogic optimism of the contributors largely prevented multiple authorship from introducing marked ideological divergences between essays. As a reference work, the 1976 Tate volume had difficulties; the coverage of topics was avowedly selective, some essay topics overlapped, and there was no index (something put right for Tate's second edition). Certainly, given the breadth of topics it covered, there was no chance of giving comprehensive coverage or even brief mention of all previously published material about each topic, and the widespread feeling by the mid-1970s that composition had changed meant that most older research or comment, or research done from different perspectives, would have seemed irrelevant anyway. By continuing the review-essay format, the volume was free to shape and consolidate composition as an independent field of study, distinct from the border disciplines of linguistics, education, and English.

Of course, all cumulative or retrospective print-bibliographies, whatever their format, have a cut-off date, after which they stop adding new coverage and go to press. Most established disciplines provide serial updatings of recently published scholarship. The 1963 NCTE report and Tate's 1976 volume can each be linked to such a serial bibliography. The 1963 focus on empirical research led to the founding of a new journal, *Research in the Teaching of English,* which has provided since 1967 a twice-yearly list of research studies and reports, while through the 1970s the Tate volume could be conveniently supplemented by Richard L. Larson's annual list in *College Composition and Communication* (covering from 1973–78, appearing in *CCC*'s May issues 1975–79). Unlike the serial bibliographies in most other disciplines, both the *RTE* and Larson's *CCC* bibliographies were selective and soon both provided annotations to each item—that is, both serial bibliographies shared the user-orientation of their cumulative precursors.

These two prototypes and their serial counterparts set the continuing character of composition bibliography—immediate usefulness, a strong sense of audience, a wish to explain the field to newcomers, a readiness to sort out, through selection and its corollary, exclusion, which items were worth continuing attention from the constant stream of new and often ephemeral publications. Yet the pattern had its limitations as well as its strengths. With the best intentions, unsympathetic or contradictory viewpoints often got further marginalized by being bibliographically invisible, while the expository treatment of sympathetic or accepted positions could be relatively uncritical. The review-essayist's ability to shape a field—the experimental focus of the 1963 report and *RTE,* the humanistic focus of Tate's contributors—gave to the emerging field first confidence and then a coherent identity, but at some cost in complexity. The dominance of this single bibliographical genre, and its serial counterpart the selective annotated list, to some degree preempted or deferred the ideological and philosophical debates that would resurface once the field gained in numbers and in institutional recognition.

Current Resources for Research on Composition

By the early 1980s, the pioneering research-reviews discussed above were getting outdated, and in any case the genre of the "orientatory essay" was becoming unrealistic for so fast developing a field. There had been enormous growth in writing about composition; new scholars entered the field, new journals were founded, and, on a conservative estimate, there had been a tenfold increase in the number of items annually published.[5] Compositionists were now interested in a much greater diversity of topics and approaches, which added to the difficulty of timely and even-handed prose review or fair selectivity in serial listing.

Paradoxically, the increasing size and complexity of the field, and the sustained influx of newcomers sharpened the need for bibliographical resources that could select from or make sense of material that would otherwise be overwhelming. One widely distributed selective list has been *The Bedford Bibliography for Teachers of Writing,* ed. Robert Gorrell, Patricia Bizzell, and Bruce Herzberg (1984; 2nd ed., 1987), which in its first edition had fewer than 200 entries but gave essay-by-essay breakdowns of many collections from the 1970s and added a very helpful brief introductory essay reviewing developments in rhetoric from classical to modern times. Similarly stringent in coverage were such single-author interpretative reviews as James Berlin's *Rhetoric and Reality* (Carbondale: Southern Illinois UP, 1987) or Stephen North's *The Making of Knowledge in Composition* (Upper Montclair, NJ: Boynton/Cook, 1987), which attempted to "map" the broad contours of the field. But useful though they often are, such selective works can hardly, by themselves, provide adequate bibliographical guidance for more experienced scholars or an adequate basis for planning longer-term research.

The best single starting-place, for orientation or reference, at least on general college composition, is now the revised or second edition of Tate's *Teaching Composition* (1987). The new version retains the original's orientatory function, with paragraph-length summaries and generous quotation from important items, but it has been significantly updated and expanded, and the essays have become more inclusive in coverage and markedly more prodigal of brief references (sometimes with three or more recent items grouped in a single end-of-paragraph parenthesis). To the original ten chapters have been added new essays on writing evaluation and on computers and writing, both technical topics that by their very difference foreground the more unified humanistic and pedagogic emphasis of the first edition. The shift from introductory orientation to a more inclusive reference function is exemplified by the provision of a detailed and very useful index of subjects and proper names; it is usually through this subject-index, rather than through the table of contents, that one should first try to identify the central material when starting work on a composition topic.

The changed scale and complexity of the field is shown also by the three hefty "bibliographic sourcebooks" published by Greenwood Press from 1984 onwards, which are now the natural starting-point for finding more detailed reviews on special topics in composition research or debate. There are three volumes in the series: *Research in Composition and Rhetoric,* edited by Michael G. Moran and Ronald F. Lunsford (1984), *Research in Technical Communication,* edited by Moran and Debra Journet (1985), and *Research in Basic Writing,* ed. Moran and Martin Jacobi (1990). The Greenwood Press volumes are compilations of review-essays by various contributors, on the established Tate model, and at first sight they just seem more elaborate and inclusive versions of their prototype; indeed the editors of the first Greenwood Press volume deliberately steered their contributors clear of most topics that had been treated in Tate's first edition, as if their effort were merely a supplement to it.

But the effect of surveying composition, not in one volume of ten chapters, but in three volumes with over fifty chapters, is to demonstrate just how much the field has changed and diversified. The essays mention many more items in each page of discussion, and each chapter concludes with a substantial reference list for further reading. The biggest shift, however, is not simply in scale, but in the kinds of topics that get chapter-length discussion—everything from writing anxiety to vocabulary, from cognitive psychology and philosophy and literary theory to usage manuals and punctuation and the teaching of legal writing. Though many essays are very readable, no one is likely to read through the three volumes, as one can read (in a sitting) through the 1963 NCTE report that started it all, and as one can still read (more episodically) through the Tate volume. No single reader is going to find every specialized topic relevant or interesting—the field isn't that coherent any more. Only the most committed individual scholar is going to buy books that cost this much; these are not impulse buys for the average conference-goer, but serious library reference purchases. Yet even reference tools this extensive (and expensive) are still generously selective shapings, rather than comprehensive records, of the published material on composition. Like the revised Tate, the Greenwood Press volumes have become essential orientation and reference tools, especially on the more technical and linguistic composition scholarship.

Both Tate and the Greenwood Press volumes make us uneasily aware of a new problem, apparently intrinsic to the essay genre as it copes with the publishing growth in composition studies. Some of the most readable contributions are those that present strongly evaluative reviews of a few major issues, perhaps ranging widely in reference but by no means attempting to "cover" all the recent professional publication on the topic; one thinks of John Warnock's opening essay on "The Writing Process" in the first Greenwood Press volume. However, once the contributor tries to be more inclusive in coverage, the references multiply, the discussion of each gets briefer, and any commentary that aspires to fairness also becomes rather bland; more and more ideas or studies get mentioned per page, but the reader gets less and less direction in deciding their relative validity, and it is, after all, that direction that justifies using the essay format in the first place.

The third recent bibliographic guide tackles this problem of evaluation head-on. It is also, significantly, a single-author text. This is George Hillocks Jr.'s *Research on Written Composition* (Urbana, IL: NCRE/ERIC, 1986). Hillocks' purpose was to survey research on composition teaching since the 1963 report, and he shares with that predecessor an emphasis on empirical or experimental work, as well as retaining its openness to research done on writing at the elementary or secondary level.

Hillocks and his assistants found references to over 6000 relevant items in various education indexes, and, after examining them, they analyzed for the survey some 2000 (including many unpublished dissertations and project reports); much of this material had not previously come to the attention of compositionists based in college English departments and is not duplicated in Tate or the Greenwood Press volumes (just as more theoretical or philosophical discussion is not covered in Hillocks). Typical titles for the kind of study Hillocks surveys might be (for a dissertation) "A Comparison of the Effectiveness of Two Grouping Plans for Teaching Community College First-Semester Freshman English Composition" or (more enticingly, for an article) "The Structure of Children's Compositions: Developmental and Ethnic Differences."

Hillocks' most distinctive innovation over the earlier report, however, lies in his much debated "meta-analysis." Meta-analysis is an attempt to reassess the validity of apparently conflicting research results on the most heavily researched topics by cross-tabulating nearly 100 additional factors from each report, even if these factors were not part of the report's own focus. Thus, Hillocks checks any variables in class activities or in the duration of the experiment, even when a study is reporting findings about the effectiveness of different essay assignments or teacher-feedback. It is hard to know quite how effective the meta-analysis is (most reviewers blenched), and some of the classifications (for example, in chapter 4 on "Modes of Instruction") seem arbitrary, but Hillocks' summaries are nonetheless quite informative, and it is well indexed. It is the most-up-to-date survey, for instance, of experimental studies on grammar and writing. Clearly the Hillocks volume aspired to be a definitive report on the state of knowledge in the field, yet one of its chief values is as a convenient index to (and cumulated list of) *RTE*- or ERIC-type materials since the early 1960s.

These three resources can, of course, be supplemented by a large number of special-topic bibliographies and bibliographic essays, often published in article form or distributed through the ERIC system. Such specialized resources can be discovered through mention in one of the general volumes discussed in this section or through the ordinary serial indexes.[6] It must, however, be kept in mind that specialized bibliographies are only as good as the search they were based on, and that they raise particular problems of search-definition—we are almost forced to define a topic as the compiler did; they are best used for preliminary orientation to a topic, or for refreshing our sense of the range of material, rather than as a substitute or short-cut for our own systematic library search early in a major project.

Current Resources for Research in Historical Rhetoric

The bibliographical situation in historical rhetoric has never been as difficult as that in modern composition studies, partly because historical rhetoricians can make more use of general tools in historical bibliography, partly because they can index things by proper names rather than by slippery subject-categories, and partly because the overlap of interest between historical rhetoric and such well-established neighboring disciplines as speech, literature, and philosophy has meant that their bibliographies have often done duty for rhetoric research also. One of the best bibliographical resources on primary materials in rhetoric was, in fact, planned as part of a multivolume bibliography of English grammar texts; the regular selective listing of new publications in the field was edited from a philosophy department; while the standard reprint-series of historical rhetoric texts was published to meet needs in speech communication.[7] However, the 1980s saw the provision of two bibliographical tools specially planned for historical rhetoricians working from a composition perspective.

The first to appear was Winifred Bryan Horner's *Historical Rhetoric: An Annotated Bibliography* (1980). This work gives both selected primary entries (including translations and modern reprints) and very full listings of secondary scholarship; its especial strength is that it lists secondary work on historical figures from speech and composition journals, not just from journals in classics or literature. The secondary material is awkwardly arranged, but it is well indexed and provides useful brief introductory essays to each of the five period-sections

(Classical, Medieval, Renaissance, Eighteenth Century, and Nineteenth Century).

More up to date, and in many ways easier to use, was a second new book, also edited by Horner. A collection of bibliographic essays, *The Present State of Scholarship in Historical and Contemporary Rhetoric* (1983) basically covers the same five periods, with several of the same contributors, but adds a chapter on twentieth-century rhetorical theory (by James Kinneavy). The essays give very useful orientations to the commonly discussed general issues in each period, and the extensive (unannotated) reference lists after each chapter are helpfully classified and subdivided.

These new tools in historical rhetoric, and especially the second, served to move the long-established field of historical rhetoric nearer to the concerns and perspectives of modern composition teachers; further evidence of the same development is the space given to historical rhetoric in the *Bedford Bibliography*. The interpretative emphasis in both Horner volumes is similar to that in the bibliographical review-volumes in modern composition, where multifarious materials are being shaped and selected to help relative newcomers to the field (indeed, *The Present State* makes a readable and helpful introductory textbook). The volumes contain plenty of material for writing a course-paper or planning a class on an historical topic, but for original research one must then go on to either specialist period-bibliographies or to general bibliographical reference tools.[8] The very urge to be helpful, to shape a new field, that motivated the new volumes makes them better as orientatory aids than as long-term comprehensive indexes to scholarship from differing disciplinary perspectives. What is also very evident, of course, is that before the 1980s, although a lot of research had been going on in historical rhetoric, there were no equivalent guides through the scholarship; Horner's two volumes made bibliographically manifest a new sense of identity, a new pattern of disciplinary affiliation, in a field that had previously tended to look to literary criticism or speech, rather than composition, for its major scholarly precursors and even for its audience.

Serial Bibliography in Composition and Rhetoric

These new and updated discursive review-volumes from the 1980s have greatly improved bibliographical guidance in both modern composition and historical rhetoric. More serious, and more difficult to solve, has been the underlying problem of what librarians call bibliographical control—the provision of a basic and inclusive year-by-year bibliographical record. Such a serial list is absolutely essential in any discipline, both to identify material published since the retrospective volumes' various cut-off dates, and to provide the basic factual information for tracking and retrieving published material through the library system. The previous *ad hoc* and selective listings, useful at the time, were no substitute for an inclusive annual record, and in any case Larson's *CCC* list was suspended after its 1978 coverage-year (while he took over the duties of *CCC* editor).

Not only was the quantity of relevant publication far outpacing the older selective lists, but during the later 1970s, the field as a whole had been shifting its boundaries, with bibliographical repercussions. As long as "composition" had meant "the teaching of (college) writing," most items would turn up in one of the two education serials, the commercially produced *Education Index,* which indexes journal items rapidly and stretches back well before most other indexes, or the massive federally funded ERIC database, which combines two print-form serials, the *Current Index to Journals in Education,* covering articles, and *Resources in Education,* covering research reports, monographs, selected conference papers, etc. Similarly, strictly linguistic aspects of composition were usually covered in the linguistic database, *Language and Language Behavior Abstracts.* The education serials especially, published monthly and then cumulated, remain essential tools for composition researchers. But as compositionists broadened their focus to cover the mental processes and social components of writing in nonpedagogic settings, the education indexes recorded only part of what was being done.

The problem of basic bibliographical control was not easy to solve, because it criss-crossed so many of the developments (and insecurities) of the new discipline.[9] Because composition is a mission-centered field, rather than one based on a single theoretical approach, it is very difficult to make a clear demarcation on subject-grounds alone of what exactly should or should not be included in a composition bibliography; for instance, does a study of a literary author's worksheets, or a management report on journalists' workhabits, belong to the field? Second, because compositionists have always written for varied audiences, their ideas have quite often been published in typically non-research formats—everything from columns in local newsletters to teachers' manuals for freshman textbooks. Much of this material never even gets into the Library of Congress. How does a bibliographer decide what is worth listing for posterity and what is simply ephemeral? Decisions about both field demarcation and formats covered need to be made on a consistent basis from item to item and year to year, so that users can predict what the bibliography has covered. Third, and most embarrassing, there was right into the 1980s little initiative from the relevant professional organizations to get anything done about composition bibliography. Even star-studded symposia about trends in the field are simply no substitute for basic informational services, yet those who take the most active part in conference-based professional organizations like MLA or NCTE have sometimes seemed reluctant to pay more than lip-service to composition's development as a research discipline, perhaps because the development itself threatens the concordat of the later 1970s, by which compositionists had won a new but almost exclusively teaching-based recognition within "English."[10] So a disciplinary bibliography of record threatened some professional identities and was closely involved in how other ones were being redefined.

What broke the deadlock was a new serial composition bibliography, Erika Lindemann's *CCCC Bibliography of Composition and Rhetoric*. This project originated independently of either professional organization, under the aegis of a farsighted commercial publisher, Longman (its original title was the *Longman Bibliography . . .)*, but it drew on an impressive number of individual compositionists as its contributors, and it is now officially linked with the NCTE's Conference on College Composition and Communication. It covers material published from 1984 onwards, thus ensuring a reasonable overlap with the cut-off or end dates for coverage in the Tate or Greenwood Press retrospective volumes.

The *CCCC Bibliography* differs from the previous annual bibliographies in the new clarity with which Lindemann defines what exactly is to be surveyed (see the extensive preface to each volume). For the first time, the *CCCC Bibliography* gives composition researchers the assurance of systematic coverage of items from a stated list of journals; inclusion or exclusion of an item no longer rests solely on the *ad hoc* decision of an individual bibliographer but on the highly mediated decision of journal editors and referees about its relevance to a recognizably composition-directed readership. The new bibliography also broadens the format-coverage from previous lists by including dissertations and conference papers distributed through ERIC, and provides comprehensive coverage of ERIC papers from the relevant core professional meetings (such as the CCCC). Each entry is supplied with a brief paragraph of descriptive annotation. The emphasis on predictability of coverage and on relative objectivity in annotation mark the bibliography as aiming to serve fellow-researchers now and in the future by compiling a record of long-term reference usefulness, a real change of purpose from earlier composition bibliography. The result is a pretty accurate reflection of a full range of research activity and discussion within modern composition studies.

Of course, by comparison with earlier composition bibliographies, these double-columned volumes with almost 2000 entries each year don't look particularly user-friendly, and subject-classification in a large-scale print-form bibliography is an intractable problem. Unlike the old Larson listing from the 1970s, the *CCCC Bibliography* is divided under subject-headings, and subdivided, with the subject classification getting more refined in successive volumes. There is also a comprehensive name index to each volume (including authors of individual essays from essay collections), but no subject index until 1987, although the generous cross-referencing at the end of each subsection somewhat compensates for this. Researchers need to follow up these cross-references fully and should be prepared to look in more than one subject-section.

Some of the subsections can run to many pages, yet further subdivision of the categories could be counter-productive, because one would end up with either a false selectivity or too many cross-references to look up. As the cross-references indicate, many articles could already go in more than one category. Instead of getting frustrated with this unavoidable fact about composition bibliography, it is worth asking what it tells us about the field.

Researchers coming into composition from literary history have, in a way, been spoilt in their expectations of what an annual bibliography can do, because the traditional literary serials (the MLA's *International Bibliography* and the MHRA's *Annual Bibliography*) could classify virtually everything under the literary author's name; something either is about Author X or it isn't, and there's only one place to look for relevant items. Composition bibliographers don't have that easy a way out. Compositionists tend to talk about more than one topic in an article, and to raise issues that cut across simple subject-categorization. However, because of the ease of proper-name categorization, literary bibliographers, until very recently, simply repressed any attempt to let scholars track material by subject (say, parallel discussions of ironic voice in two texts of different periods, or applications of the same theoretical perspective to dissimilar texts). Historical rhetoricians face a similar problem. It is much easier to find everything written about, say, Richard Whately, than to find all recent discussion of a theoretical issue Whately treated (like, say, the variety of rhetorical openings; even if there were an historical subject-index, "rhetorical openings" might also be indexed as "introductions" or "exordia" or dealt with under such topics as voice or ethos or relation to audience).

Whole generations of literary and rhetorical scholarship (especially in dissertation research) were channeled away from general or theoretical issues, at least in part, by the nature of bibliographical indexing in their fields. Even since 1981, when the MLA introduced subject-classifications alongside the traditional author-classification, subject-searching in literary research is still a very frustrating prospect. The new fourth volume ("General") of the MLA *Annual Bibliography,* which has to deal with the subject-dependent field of critical theory (and, incidentally, the teaching of writing), provides the real parallel to the problems a composition bibliographer faces, and that volume is notoriously difficult to use, with overlapping categorizations and page after page of underdifferentiated and unannotated entries. Subject-classification is an intrinsically difficult problem, but at least composition bibliography has fully recognized that the problem exits, and is tackling it about as well as is possible in print-form or hard-copy.

However, logically, the problem of bibliographical compilation (or "control") is prior to and distinct from the problem of subject-indexing (or "retrieval"); the importance of the *CCCC Bibliography* is in breaking the deadlock on the first of these problems. The problem of retrieval is one that is only worth solving once a discipline has a decent comprehensive and systematic record of publications to retrieve from. The very existence of a serious annual bibliographical record should have the effect both of stabilizing and pluralizing the field—stabilizing it, because it provides composition scholars with new opportunities to build responsibly on the work of their predecessors, and pluralizing it, because researchers now face the full range of contemporary discussion on a topic, rather than a preselected subset of what has been published. It is an historic development for composition studies, which deserves compositionists' ongoing cooperation.

Some Concluding Observations and Some Practical Advice

Implicit in the discussion so far has been the close connection between bibliographical developments and other changes (both epistemological and generational) within the discipline. For twenty years or so, composition bibliography has tried to bridge two functions—rhetorically, it promised to communicate neutral information (what was known, or what had been published), while in format it foregrounded the value-preemptive functions of mapping and interpretation. With quantitative growth in the field, and with the maturing of the composition bibliographer's target-audience from neophytes to trained specialist, it has become almost impossible satisfactorily to combine these two functions.

The necessary shift in composition bibliography toward the first function, the creation of a bibliographical record, has meant a shift from constructing the field in ideological terms (around a theoretical paradigm) toward a socially mediated definition (from the coalition of professional groupings); bibliographically, "composition" now means, not what some individual Humpty-Dumpty-like bibliographer says it ought to mean, but "what composition journals publish, and what composition conferences accept."

This shift has in recent years brought to attention two aspects of the field that the earlier interpretative guides had tended to downplay. First, the new bibliographies confirm that scholarly activity in composition is highly audience-directed. Even when their writing is rigorously grounded (and much that gets disseminated is still not especially rigorous), compositionists deliberately utilize a variety of publication formats perhaps more typical of the professional schools than of traditional humanities researchers. At its best, this audience-relatedness has been a strength, providing a kind of dialectic between specialized or theoretical work and practical, common-sense, discipline-wide perspectives. In some ways, such generic variety parallels, in its strengths and weaknesses, the dialectic between theory and classroom practice of the teacher-researcher movement; both are easy to dismiss or underestimate and equally easy to sentimentalize, but both represent something central to the nature of modern composition studies. Publication format is hardly an adequate basis for separating the scholarly wheat from the inspirational chaff, so users of composition bibliographies must become more than usually careful that the purpose for which they cite a publication is consistent with its character.

Second, the new composition bibliographies have exposed for the first time the full methodological and ideological diversity within the field. In the 1970s, "process theory" could be put forward as a single, comprehensive, and coherent approach to the field. Inadequate bibliographical records, and well-intentioned ideologically based selectivity by the bibliographical guides, either rendered other perspectives invisible or marginalized dissentient voices by labeling them as outmoded, unbalanced, and underinformed. Of course, any human activity can be studied from a number of theoretical perspectives, and the dominance of a single theoretical paradigm is a function, not just of heuristic power, but of social pressures within the professional community (in this case, compositionists' need in the 1970s for professional differentiation and cohesion). The selective and orientatory bibliographical guides helped compositionists achieve this differentiation and cohesion. By the 1980s, with the new acceptance of composition within universities, these pressures had diminished. The demographic growth of the composition research community during the 1980s has not only permitted sub-specialization but has also revealed a continuing if long-repressed diversity of intellectual perspective.

This diversity does not necessarily presage the fragmentation of the composition movement. After all, such fields as psychology or literature or history or linguistics do not rest on a single theoretical perspective. To some degree, the new socially based composition bibliographies, which in effect do not make judgments for or against an item's soundness of approach, are more likely than the older guides to hold the field together. Simply listing the diverse material together should help scholars gain a healthy mutual understanding of what other approaches are out there.

However, the improved resources for bibliographical control have not been matched by equal improvement in aids for searching the bibliographical record. We are much better off than we were, but, as the old library-school saw puts it, our capacity to compile information has far outstripped our ability to retrieve it. The considerable bibliographical resources we now have are not being well used. To some extent, the responsibility lies with graduate programs; few graduate departments give adequate instruction in the special bibliographical problems of composition.[11] To some extent, as the discussion above has indicated, difficulty in subject-searching is intrinsic to a field with shifting boundaries and changing terminology.[12] But the problem also comes from researchers bringing to the search process surprisingly traditional and rigid ideas of what bibliographies do and surprisingly passive ideas about how bibliographical data should be handled.

Practical advice about composition bibliography must therefore be concerned with attitudes and search-strategies, not just with the bibliographies themselves. Often, for instance, when quite sophisticated composition graduate students turn to a bibliographical search, they revert to the worst kind of old-style high-school-research-paper thinking and assume that, given the right subject-heading and the right bibliography, they ought to find readymade *the* list of all necessary material. This could only be true if the research project was a first-level search on a very stable aspect of the discipline. As compositionists should know, research-writing (and therefore research) is not simply about assembling readymade information, but about changing the ways a topic can be looked at and about making new cross-connections between material. These transformations are as necessary in bibliographical research as in any other kind; the bibliographical record is only the discrete raw material within which the individual researcher makes the cross-connections. Part of any extensive search-process is to break out of or to evade the bibliographies' own prior categorizations of material.

Experienced researchers get full use out of bibliographical resources by search-strategies that maximize their own active, choosing role, rather than the bibliographer's prepackaged selections. They will often initiate or supplement a formal library-search by tapping into the oral network—talking to colleagues, picking the brains of mentors, attending conference sessions, and even by making phone inquiries to likely specialists. They look over several of the introductory research guides to see if their topic might have been fitted into the taxonomy of the discipline in more than one way or discussed under more than one label. They give themselves time for the serendipitous browsing of recent journals and of the relevant library shelves. None of these strategies is a substitute for a formal library-search, but each can tap a researcher into items (and subject categories) that will improve it.

There is a difference, too, between the experienced and inexperienced researcher in the handling of the hard-copy or print-form bibliographies that are the basis of most library research. First, experienced researchers spend time familiarizing themselves with the scope and arrangement of any bibliographical tool before using it for a search. Then, they get the best results from almost any composition bibliography by checking several different subject categories, not just a single heading. Rather than trying to narrow their search to find exactly the right material the first time, they will do better by scanning broad categories with far more titles or abstracts than they will ultimately need. For most purposes, it is better to use multiple bibliographical sources rather than relying on a single favorite source—not just because a favorite source might exclude relevant items (different bibliographies have different methodological leanings, for instance), but because in any particular source all the relevant items may not be sorted or indexed under the headings(s) the researcher is using. And experienced researchers do not expect to carry through a project in straightforward linear fashion; bibliographical searching, reading, and writing, interact with one another throughout a research project.

Increased opportunities for making these active cross-connections in the scholarly record have come with the improved availability of relevant bibliographies in database form for computer searching. These databases are not a magic answer—they can never be better than the bibliographical records they assemble—and a computer-search often gives a beginner a false sense of security that he or she has "got everything," but every composition researcher should get used to using the available databases fully. Many scholars still treat the databases as convenient computerized versions of print-form subject-bibliographies, but actually they allow quite new kinds of searching. For the present, the database with which compositionists are most familiar is the mammoth ERIC system (the acronym stands for the federal Education Resources Information Center, founded in 1966), though recent years of *Education Index* are also available in database. ERIC provides very elaborate subject-indexing under a special set of indexing terms, published as the *Thesaurus of ERIC Descriptors*. By combining several of these descriptors, one can retrieve the subset of relevant items within quite broad subject categories, and most major libraries provide help in designing such a search.

The cost of on-line searching has inhibited most humanities-based researchers from moving beyond this basic use of the database, but with the widespread recent distribution of ERIC and *Education Index* on CD-ROM, where the cost is carried by the library rather than by the individual user, it becomes practical to use the databases more flexibly. The real possibilities of database searches come when, instead of the system's formal subject-headings, one uses free-text searching, the equivalent of a perfect concordance or of a very fast eagle-eyed page-by-page scan through the whole bibliography. Free-text searching (either alone or in combination with a descriptor) can pick out the titles and abstracts that contain any specified combination of words or phrases. The researcher can manipulate the database over and over again, playing through variants and synonyms, in search patterns never anticipated by those who set up the system or designed its indexing terms. Free-text searching works best when, like ERIC, but unlike the *MLA International Bibliography,* the database includes abstracts, not just titles, and a free-text search is particularly useful for picking up items on some new topic or approach for which ERIC does not yet have a special descriptor. The *CCCC Bibliography* has already been prepared (for editing and production purposes) in electronic form, and in due course, as it builds up coverage over a longer time-span, it may become economic for that *CCCC* working database to become available to researchers, at least on-line.

Along with the well-known education bibliographies, a second kind of more general database can help researchers circumvent the difficulty of subject-categorization in composition. This is the citation index, essentially a list, item by item, of recent articles in a specified range of journals that have cited or footnoted a specific publication.[13] Citation indexes were developed in the sciences, and they work better in journal-based disciplines than in disciplines (such as literature) that rely on monograph publication, because monographs would be too cumbersome to index in this way. At its most original, modern composition scholarship has been largely journal-centered, and citation indexes therefore hold great possibilities. They let us track articles, not by topic, but by intellectual affiliation. We might, for instance, pick out every recent article that cited a particular essay by Kenneth Burke, whatever the article's ostensible subject. Nor are the citation-indexes limited to use with influential major texts. One way to approach the search for recent scholarship on a composition topic is to select a couple of articles on the topic that are now some five or ten years old (by using Tate or Moran and Lunsford), and then to see which subsequent writers have cited those articles; if we then look back at the other sources these subsequent writers were citing, we have quickly built up a fairly dense record of scholarly activity on our chosen topic, but without ever relying on the slippery selectivity of traditional subject-indexes.

Citation-searching is an ideal method for exploring scholarly discus-

sion on tricky theoretical issues, because it picks up on webs of intellectual relationship in a way that scanning essay titles in a bibliography
would never do. Good citation-searches in composition require the use
of both the *Arts and Humanities Citation Index* and the *Social Science
Citation Index,* each covering a different range of relevant journals.
Though only the latter is currently available on CD-ROM, both are
available on-line, and in any case, since people usually search citations
of a few items over a short time-period, hard-copy searches are not that
cumbersome once they understand the citation-index format.

For many years, composition bibliography has been regarded as a
kind of poor relation, trying belatedly and amateurishly to catch up with
the superior bibliographical resources in more established fields. The
1980s have given compositionists several much improved retrospective
guides to composition scholarship and a superior annual bibliography of
record. But the 1980s have also shown that compositionists should not
simply be replicating (or hoping someone else will replicate) the bibliographical patterns of other disciplines. What may seem to English-
based researchers the special problems of bibliography in composition—the field's protean nature, its multiple theoretical affiliations, and
the diverse audiences that occasion its publications—make composition
typical of much modern humanistic scholarship; in many ways, it is
more representative than the older literary-historical scholarship in
which most compositionists received their only formal bibliographical
training. Compositionists, like researchers in most fields, can still learn
from traditional reference specialists (particularly about general bibliographical resources, which are underused in composition). However,
by and large, when composition researchers struggle seriously with the
information-retrieval problems of their field, they have moved beyond
the rather rudimentary and simplistic search methods that commonly
suffice for the analogous problems in current literary criticism. Compositionists need to realize that their field poses real bibliographical
difficulties, but they should no longer feel apologetic about how the
composition community has been tackling them.

To anatomize composition through its bibliographical resources may
seem somewhat reductive, like using a two-dimensional X ray to explain human beings, while neglecting everything that might be added by
anthropologists or philosophers or molecular-biological theorists or historians of human evolution, let alone by middle managers and professional lobbyists. But the newer composition bibliographies provide an

unusually clear picture of just how composition has matured and developed as a discipline. It is a much more complex picture than used to be painted during the great growth period of the 1970s; composition is a much more creatively heterogeneous discipline. This heterogeneity long made it difficult to design appropriate bibliographical tools, but the same heterogeneity is what makes composition bibliographically interesting. Perhaps it is also the source of the field's continuing intellectual interest.

Notes

1. Earlier resources, including bibliographical tools in border disciplines, are described in Patrick Scott and Bruce Castner, "Reference Sources for Composition Research: A Practical Survey," *College English* 45 (December 1983): 756–68.

2. The classic protest is Paul Bryant's "A Brand New World Every Morning," *College Composition and Communication* 25 (February 1974): 30–35.

3. Thomas S. Kuhn, *The Structure of Scientific Revolutions* (Chicago: U of Chicago P, 1962): 136.

4. (Champaign, IL: National Council of Teachers of English, 1963).

5. On composition journals, see the evaluative review by Robert J. Connors, "Journals in Composition Studies," *College English* 46 (April 1984): 348–65, or the two enumerative lists by Chris M. Anson: "A Computerized List of Journals Publishing Articles in Composition," *College Composition and Communication* 37 (May 1986): 154–66, and (with Hildy Miller), "Journals in Composition: An Update," *College Composition and Communication* 39 (May 1988): 198–216. The estimate of tenfold growth comes from comparing Larson's annual *CCC* list from the mid-1970s with Lindemann's *Longman Bibliography* (see below) from ten years later; some of the increase could be explained as the more comprehensive bibliographical coverage in Lindemann.

6. A useful short list of special-topic bibliographies is section 2 of Bizzell and Herzberg, *Bedford Bibliography,* or see Scott and Castner, pp. 763–64. On serial bibliographies, see sections below.

7. Robin C. Alston, *A Bibliography of the English Language from the Invention of Printing to the Year 1800* (Leeds: Arnold, 1965–72, rev. 1974), esp. vol. 6 "Rhetoric . . ."; "Current Bibliography of Books on Rhetoric," in *Rhetoric Society Newsletter* (later *Rhetoric Society Quarterly*), edited from the Philosophy Department, St. Cloud University, MN; and the Southern Illinois UP reprint series, Landmarks in Rhetoric and Public Address.

8. For a list of relevant general reference tools, and period bibliographies in

historical rhetoric, see Scott and Castner pp. 757–61; note also a revised second edition of James J. Murphy, *Medieval Rhetoric, A Selective Bibliography* (Toronto: U of Toronto P, 1989), and Forrest Houlette, *Nineteenth-Century Rhetoric, An Enumerative Bibliography* (New York: Garland, 1989). On the application of technical (textual) bibliography in historical rhetoric, cf. Patrick Scott, "The Textual Basis of Rhetorical Research: Some Bibliographical Questions," *Rhetoric Society Quarterly* 14 (1984): 43–52.

9. On these issues, cf. Patrick Scott, "Bibliographical Problems in Research on Composition," *College Composition and Communication* 37 (May 1986): 167–77.

10. In justice, throughout this period NCTE was sponsoring the relevant ERIC Clearinghouse, and thus was supporting the bibliographical needs of its general membership, if not the special needs of composition scholars.

11. Ten years ago, surveys showed a total neglect of composition sources in English graduate bibliography courses and research guides; see *Literary Research Newsletter* 4 (Winter 1979): 3–41, and *College English* 44 (April 1982): 392. Since then, there are signs of at least some improvement: see, e.g., Thomas M. Gage and John C. Schafer, in *WPA: Writing Program Administration* 7 (Spring 1984): 29; Scott and Castner, as in note 1 above; John Fenstermaker, in *Literary Research Newsletter* 7 (Winter 1982): 9; and the inclusion of a section on composition reference sources in the latest edition of the MLA's *Literary Research Guide,* ed. James L. Harner (New York: Modern Language Association 1989), 585–92.

12. Cf. Scott, "Bibliographical Problems," pp. 167–70.

13. My understanding of what citation indexes offer to composition research owes much to an imaginative project by Robert E. Smith, tracing the debate among technical writing specialists over an article of Carolyn Miller's.

Suggested Readings

Bizzell, Patricia, and Bruce Herzberg. *The Bedford Bibliography for Teachers of Writing.* 3rd ed. Boston: Bedford, 1991.

Hillocks, George, Jr. *Research on Written Composition: New Directions for Teaching.* Urbana, IL: National Conference on Research in English and ERIC, 1986.

Horner, Winifred Bryan, ed. *Historical Rhetoric: An Annotated Bibliography of Selected Sources in English.* Boston: G. K. Hall, 1980.

———. *The Present State of Scholarship in Historical and Contemporary Rhetoric.* Rev. ed. Columbia: U of Missouri P, 1990.

Lindemann, Erika, ed. *CCCC Bibliography of Composition and Rhetoric [1987–].* Carbondale: Southern Illinois UP, 1990– . Continues the original title, also edited by Erika Lindemann, *Longman Bibliography of Composition and Rhetoric [1984–86]*. New York: Longman, 1987–88.

Moran, Michael, and Martin J. Jacobi, eds. *Research in Basic Writing: A Bibliographic Sourcebook*. Westport, CT: Greenwood, 1990.

Moran, Michael, and Debra G. Journet, eds. *Research in Technical Communication: A Bibliographic Sourcebook*. Westport, CT: Greenwood, 1985.

Moran, Michael G., and Ronald F. Lunsford, eds. *Research in Composition and Rhetoric: A Bibliographic Sourcebook*. Westport, CT: Greenwood, 1984.

Tate, Gary, ed. *Teaching Composition: Twelve Bibliographical Essays*. Fort Worth: Texas Christian UP, 1987.

Research in Composition: Issues and Methods

Lillian Bridwell-Bowles

UNIVERSITY OF MINNESOTA

Within the composition community we have some disagreements about research that we can trace back to Plato and Aristotle, with aggravations added by Descartes, Bacon, Locke, and others ever since. They center around reality and ways of knowing. Does objective reality (i.e., "truth") exist? And if so, how can it be apprehended? If it exists, does it exist apart from the language used to describe it? In composition studies, we welcome a range of answers to these questions and a range of theoretical and methodological positions, as our journals attest.[1] Nevertheless, we have a long and clear history of favoring social scientific methods for research and a more recent and cloudy history of welcoming into the research community more philosophical, naturalistic, or deconstructivist inquiries. In this chapter, I hope to provide an overview of this history and some of the explanations for our biases. I shall also outline the objects of inquiry that our research investigates, some of the major epistemological differences that have coexisted during the period from the 1960s through the 1980s within the composition research community, the major methodological approaches used, and some issues that remain to be addressed as composition research continues to evolve.

Sources for the Beginning Composition Researcher

Within the space of one essay, I cannot hope to provide a comprehensive picture of composition research, but I will cite a number of major books (Beach and Bridwell; Cooper and Odell; Lauer and Asher; North; Phelps; Hillocks; Freedman, Dyson, Flower, and Chafe; Moran and

Lunsford; Flood, Jensen, Lapp, and Squire) on the topic to supplement this chapter. Taken collectively, these sources can provide a reasonably broad view of research in our field.

Given the label Stephen North has applied to *Research in the Teaching of English (RTE)*, "the leading Researcher journal in Composition" (135), this journal is a useful one for the beginning composition specialist to examine as a case study of the modern history of composition research. Anne Herrington's article on twenty years of *RTE* provides just such a comprehensive overview from the perspective of composition studies. Even though *RTE* is not exclusively a composition journal, more composition submissions were reviewed by its editors than any other kind over the years from 1987 through 1989,[2] thus demonstrating the impact of composition research on the larger community concerned with teaching all of the English language arts. Other journals listed at the end of this article provide the primary homes for most composition research.

The Object of Inquiry; or, What Are We Studying?

Any description of research in the field depends, of course, on where we mark its beginning. Despite the obvious existence of earlier research on composition (Lyman, Hoyt), most writers mark the beginning of modern composition research with the publication of Braddock, Lloyd-Jones, and Schoer's book, *Research in Written Composition*, published in 1963. Setting this date helps us to distinguish a modern period of research, with an emphasis on empirically observable data, from other periods in which the more typical kinds of scholarship were non-empirical, intuitive or introspective, and seated in rhetoric or philosophy, rather than in social science.

Prior to this modern period, and on into the 1950s and 1960s, the sparse empirical research that existed was focused on narrow issues or segments of language. Moran and Lunsford's *Research in Composition and Rhetoric* is constructed around some of the topics that this early research frequently investigated, including separate chapters on such topics as the sentence, the paragraph, spelling, usage, and textbooks.

Various methodologies for teaching composition were a popular focus around mid-century, as revealed in the many comparisons of methodologies summarized in Braddock, Lloyd-Jones, and Schoer.

During the 1970s, many critics questioned these methodological studies, including Cooper and Odell, who characterized experimental research on teaching methodologies as "corn field studies" because of their reliance on statistical designs derived from agronomy. They and others such as Janet Emig and Martha King called for more basic research into questions about composing and the nature of texts.

Studying static products was unpopular throughout the expansionary years for composition research during the 1970s and 1980s. Instead of analyzing texts and their features, researchers began to study what Louise Phelps calls the "human science" or "psychology" of composition. Researchers wanted to know how human beings write, both behaviorally and cognitively. As I argued in 1984, "the dramatic shift came when [composition researchers] began analyzing what writers really do when they write, not what they 'ought to do' based on *a priori* logical assumptions" (3). In defining what she calls an "objectivist conception of text," Phelps lays out the history of the famed process/product opposition in composition. Among other things, the shift in priorities succeeded in "reconstituting the field as a research discipline" (132).

A myriad of process studies in the 1970s and 1980s responded to the calls for "basic research" on composing processes. Janet Emig is credited with being the first to conduct such research, and she was followed by Sommers, Perl, Bridwell, and others. Such studies examined various parts of composing processes, including invention, drafting, revising, and rereading during composing. Studies of the pedagogical technique called sentence-combining, which attempted to increase syntactic fluency without formal instruction in grammar, were also common during these decades (see Kleine for a review and critique).

Perhaps the most significant developments during the 1970s and 1980s were studies of the "cognitive" processes involved in writing introduced by Flower and Hayes. Using a technique called "protocol analysis" which was borrowed from cognitive psychology, researchers asked writers to talk aloud as they composed to gain insight into the mind at work "at the point of utterance." (See Steinberg and Dobrin for commentaries on this method.) Others used videotapes (Matsuhashi) or computer programs (Bridwell-Bowles, Johnson and Brehe; Bridwell, Sirc, and Brooke) to capture behavioral records of composing processes in minute detail. With the advent of computers into writers' workplaces came research on the effects of word processing on composing and on the effects of computer-assisted instruction (see Bridwell-Bowles, "Designing Research," for a summary of much of this work). Many of these researchers attempted to build models of the cognitive processes involved in writing as they interpreted their data.

In recent theoretical work, we have begun to recognize new research questions on the product side of the process/product dichotomy. For too long we believed that the more intriguing problems in research were on the process side. With new insights from discourse analysis (see Coulthard and van Dijk for introductions) and poststructuralist theory (see Culler for a historical introduction), it is now clear that our conceptions of text demand just as many questions. White provides an accessible summary of the effects of new theories about reading texts and how they account for our responses to writing.

Given the complex relationships and interactions among writer(s), reader(s), text(s), and culture(s), many possible readings and interpretations of a "text" are possible. As Phelps asks, "What concrete fact of experience, then, are people pointing to when they 'refer' to the structure of a given text?" (138). This question is of particular significance in writing assessment studies where theorists are beginning to question judgments of writing quality made without adequate attention to context. In fact, if we question our judgments of writing quality, we question the results of much composition research that uses quality as a variable (but more on this later).

These newly introduced theoretical problems, and many others, have led to an emphasis in the 1980s and early 1990s on studying the contexts for writing. Who is writing, in what context, for whom, for what purpose, and with what underlying assumptions? Beach and Bridwell, for example, divide their "new directions" in composition research into research on composing processes, writing situations, and instructional contexts. Ethnographic researchers have employed theories ranging from pragmatics to Marxism, feminism, and deconstructionism (see McLaren) to describe as richly as possible the circumstances for the production of written language and its possible meanings. Their methods include participant-observation, interviewing, and multiple perspectives, among others, and they produce detailed descriptions, often in narrative form.

Underlying Assumptions in Composition Research

Inevitably, any emerging field must find ways of defining itself apart from others or showing how it shares similarities and convergences with others; this is particularly true of an interdisciplinary or cross-disciplinary field such as composition studies. Another task is to outline its epistemological assumptions. As members of the composition research community have tried to define the field and its assumptions, we have discovered that composition studies is composed of a fairly loose confederation of members with differing intellectual histories, and, consequently differing perspectives on our teaching and research.

James Berlin provides us with one "map" of the conflicting positions in the field, outlining four kinds of pedagogical theorists: the Neo-Aristotelians, the Positivists or Current Traditionalists, the Neo-Platonists, and the New Rhetoricians. Even though a number of rhetoricians have disputed the rigidity of these categories, the differences he describes are useful because they offer one explanation for the various paradigms that exist within composition research. Because research in composition has been intimately linked to questions of pedagogy, differing pedagogical paradigms signal methodological debates within our research. Let us examine the underlying assumptions of these four theories.

For the Neo-Aristotelians and the Positivists, objective reality can be known through the senses, with the addition of either deductive or inductive reasoning. Language is a relatively unproblematic medium with clear connections between words and meaning. On the other hand, the Neo-Platonists and the New Rhetoricians, as Berlin describes them, believe that reality or truth must be somehow interpreted or constructed by human beings through language. Neo-Platonists believe that reality or truth is always mediated by the individual, while the New or Epistemic Rhetoricians believe that truth is constructed of the interactions among writer, audience, external phenomena, language, and culture. According to Berlin, "The New Rhetoric denies that truth is discoverable in sense impression since this data must always be interpreted—structured and organized—in order to have meaning" (774). The connections between language and meaning are far more complex for Neo-Platonists and New Rhetoricians.

Within composition research, we see similarities between Neo-Aristotelians and Positivists in the assumptions made by "quantitative" researchers. Neo-Platonists and New Rhetoricians are more similar to those we call "qualitative" researchers. Sandra Stotsky, in a very useful overview of research methodologies, provides a number of labels for the two kinds of research within our field: for "quantitative" research, she lists "positivistic," "scientific," and "hypothesis-testing" as rough synonyms; for "qualitative," she includes "holistic," "phenomenological," "hypothesis-generating," "participant-observational," "ethnographic," "humanistic," "naturalistic," "interpretivistic," and "hermeneutical," among others.

The American Educational Research Association, an organization to which some composition researchers belong, makes an additional distinction between "research" and "conceptual inquiry." The first depends on empirical data, information that can be sensed or experienced and collected, analyzed, and interpreted. The latter depends on philosophical or conceptual speculation and not on empirical data. Other writers (Myers; Bridwell and Beach) have described positivist, rationalist, and contextualist paradigms for research, leaving open the possibility of some combination of conceptualizing and data-gathering. Systems of classification that separate conceptual theorizing from "research" are characteristic of social scientific or positivist definitions of research. In more recent composition research, the more salient distinction may turn on whether or not the patterns that are perceived within empirical data are presumed to exist *a priori* or whether they are described as socially constructed by the participants and by the researcher.

In their excellent overview of empirical research in composition, Lauer and Asher include the following types of research studies: case studies, ethnographies, surveys, quantitative descriptive studies, experimental designs, and meta-analyses. Rather than using methodologies as a means of sorting research, North classifies researchers and their characteristic "modes of inquiry" into four categories: experimentalists, clinicians, formalists, and ethnographers. Both books treat research as something different from the activities of practitioners, historians, philosophers, and critics, the activities typically associated with traditional humanistic teaching or scholarship. Not surprisingly, North directly attributes much about his way of working to Deising's book entitled *Patterns of Discovery in the Social Sciences.*

North claims that practitioners are mainly interested in the question, "What do we do?" and scholars with "What does it mean?" Researchers, according to North, are supposed to ask "What happened (or happens)?" Such divisions are artificial, of course. Teachers ask questions about meaning and observations, scholars in composition studies are concerned with practice and observation, and researchers care about meaning and interpretation as well as practice. Using current deconstructionist theories, one could further argue that all science embeds certain philosophical and hermeneutical assumptions.

More recently, particularly with the borrowings of poststructuralism that we have seen in the late 1980s, there have been some shifts toward more speculative "research" that places less faith in observation or measurement, but for the most part such work is still called "conceptual" or "scholarly," and not "research." Typically, certain kinds of historians, philosophers, and critical theorists who work in composition are excluded from "research" by North, Lauer and Asher, and others because of the way the profession continues to limit its definition of research.

In most composition research, the heritage of social science is clearly revealed in the positivist belief that truth resides in reality and that reality can be observed, measured, and described so as to reveal that truth. These beliefs are clearly evident in quantitative studies, but they are also at the heart of some qualitative or ethnographic studies that interpret observations, artifacts, and relationships. The difference between a positivist and an interpretive or hermeneutical tradition for research lies in the degree to which researchers allow themselves to speculate about meaning and bias.

The facts must speak for themselves in hypothesis-testing research; either something is true or not true, within a certain range of probability. Of course, the researcher has to interpret the findings, but he or she is aware that this is mainly a *descriptive* task (i.e., describing all the possible influences on variables). Naturalistic researchers in a more hermeneutical tradition write "thick descriptions" and self-consciously interpret their data within a set of meanings that they often describe as "socially constructed." Many see their interpretations as *constructive,* rather than descriptive. They are aware of the shifts in interpretation that can take place from one observer to another. In the section on methodology, I discuss some of the ways naturalistic researchers deal with multiple realities. Of course, not all naturalistic researchers belong to the "social construction" school of thought, so it is possible that some researchers might import positivist assumptions about truth into their ethnographies, for example.

Another assumption of our research heritage is the faith that engaging in composition research can lead to solutions of certain problems, particularly pedagogical problems. This gives it a decidedly "applied," rather than "basic" or "pure" emphasis. (See Bridwell and Beach for a list of the challenges to a current-traditional pedagogy that have come from the research community.) Even during the 1970s when we heard repeated calls for "basic research" on composing processes, the emphasis was on discovering and applying this knowledge within the context of composition classrooms.

These ways of sorting out "types" of composition research and their shared assumptions, like all dichotomies and systems of classification, are often simplistic, reductive, and misleading. The members of the groups are almost never "pure types" incapable of change. All possible combinations exist (e.g., a feminist who produces critical theory as research/scholarship, but who gathers empirical data to get funds for her writing program). Some would argue that *all* research is conceptual and dependent upon a philosophical position, whether stated or unstated; that *all* reporting is interpreting; and that *all* research designs include both inductive and deductive reasoning, hypothesis-testing, and hypothesis-generating. Even those who want to maintain the boundaries between types may argue for an eclectic position that uses knowledge gained from all sources. Witte, for example, argues that composition can embrace qualitative studies and their "logic of discovery," as well as quantitative studies and their "logic of validation."

Nevertheless, because these distinctions exist within the literature on composition research, it is useful to understand the dialectical tensions they set up within the field and their consequences for emerging knowledge and theory within composition studies. More recent trends suggest that these systems of classification are becoming less rigid; for example, we routinely describe historical work as "research," especially that which examines empirical data such as writing textbooks (Connors). Moran and Lunsford, writing out of a tradition broader than many of the books on research cited above, include rhetoric, philosophy, psychology, and literary theory in their collection entitled *Research in Composition and Rhetoric*.

Methodologies: How Do We Seek Answers to Our Questions?

It should be quite apparent by now that the answer to this question is, "*very* differently." In this section, I shall try to provide a brief summary of several major types of research. For a more complete study of methodologies, please see Beach and Bridwell; Lauer and Asher; Phelps; Kantor, Kirby and Goetz; Flood, Jensen, Lapp, and Squire; and Hillocks; among others.

Quantitative Studies

EXPERIMENTAL STUDIES

Experimental designs are used most often when the researcher wants to compare one instructional methodology with another. The method depends upon severe control over the environment to insure that the "subjects" (i.e., student writers) are "randomly assigned to treatments" (i.e., experimental or controlled teaching conditions). The researcher begins with a "null hypothesis" (e.g., "There will be no significant differences between treatment A and treatment B on the criterion variable") and tests this hypothesis using statistical inference (e.g., "analysis of variance").

To translate this into "compositionese," researchers might decide to test the effects of using a particular computer software package to teach students to revise. They would want to compare results with this package to traditional methods. To insure that their statistical procedures would be valid, they would have to assign students randomly to separate groups that would get the different kinds of instruction. They might also want a "control" group that would have no instruction at all in revision. Next, they would have to determine what measure they would use to determine successful revision. A typical measure might be holistic ratings of differences in quality between first and second drafts of a paper composed by everyone in the experiment. They would then study the improvements in drafts and statistically test to see whether the variability in ratings could be systematically attributed to the treatments. They would decide this on the basis of a "probability" level that would be set in advance of the experiment. (See Lauer and Asher; Hillocks for extended explanations of experimental designs.)

The chief advantage of this kind of study is the clarity with which it is understood by the empirical research community and by consumers who like "yes/no" answers, or perhaps even "maybe" answers, so long as the degree of certainty or the percentages are reported. An argument can sometimes be made for a cause-effect relationship between treatments and outcomes, if the study is carefully conducted and if the theoretical justification behind the study is strong enough. These kinds of arguments using statistical evidence can be extremely powerful, particularly in efforts to obtain resources for costly instructional equipment or materials.

The obvious liabilities with experimental research are the artificial nature of the experiment and the lack of attention to contexts or differences within individuals. Statistical studies deal with patterns across large groups, and they depend upon controlled conditions if the assumptions upon which the statistical tests are based are to be satisfied. Classrooms and students don't often fit this model of research in the ways that rats or cornfields often do. Furthermore, good rat or cornfield researchers would never let themselves get caught with outcome variables as abstract and "ill defined" as some of the ones we have in writing (e.g., "good" writing, ability to compose). They use "speed through a maze" or "bushels per acre," variables that are easily counted or measured. Their studies do not often describe the lives of their subjects for many hours per week over several months. With such limitations, they really can "control" their experiments, unlike most composition researchers. In composition, we have difficulty grafting "soft" and subjective research questions onto an inappropriate research rhetoric from agronomy or behavioral science.

"Random assignment to treatment" illustrates one of the ways composition research often violates the assumptions behind experimental research. Students register for classes at a certain hour or in a certain location, and they may be unwilling to be assigned to other sections just to satisfy the researcher's needs. It may be very difficult to offer several different treatments within the same classroom without introducing "contamination" into the experiment. In many so-called experimental designs, the researchers assign the treatments to pre-existing classrooms, thus introducing potential bias (e.g., students in the 1:00 P.M. "control" class were sleepier than students in the 10:00 A.M. "experimental" section; somehow more honors students ended up in a particular section).

More subtle differences have to do with assuming that everything that is important is uncovered in an experimental design. The experimenter may deliberately stay out of the classroom to avoid the contamination that comes when subjects know they are being studied. Those in the classroom might be aware of all kinds of influences operating on the environment that were not a part of the formal research design (e.g., two weeks before the hypothetical study above, the students had been forced to try a poorly designed software package and had negative attitudes toward computer-assisted writing instruction). Of course, this kind of influence might be reported to the researcher who could then use it in his or her interpretations, but many times such influences are missed because of the barrier between the "researcher" and the subjects and their teachers, in the case of classroom research.

Another problem arises in assuming that the results of a particular study will apply in another context. One of the chief advantages of conducting experimental research, according to its proponents, is that we can safely "generalize" from one study to another. The irony is that so much control goes into experiments that we are unlikely ever to see the same conditions in a more natural setting. With our current interest in promoting diversity within composition, research designs predicated upon "averages" and "generalizations" may not be the method of choice. Nevertheless, many experimental studies produce results that ring true and are useful.

META-ANALYSES

Once a body of experimental (or "quasi-experimental," Lauer and Asher) research exists on a certain topic, the consumers of research are then faced with the problem of connecting results from one study to the next, particularly if the results are mixed. A technique called "meta-analysis" has become popular among social scientists because it allows investigators to blend findings from a number of studies, using special procedures for controlling certain types of statistical errors and design differences. Smith and Klein offer the following list of synthetic studies: literature review, research review, interpretive analysis, integrative review, research integration, meta-analysis, state of the art summarizing, evaluation synthesis, or best-evidence synthesis. Of these, only meta-analysis has its own rigorously defined rules for statistical analysis.

In one of the few such meta-analyses in our field, Hillocks constructed three broad categories—mode of instruction, focus of instruction, and duration of instruction—by combining results in individual investigations so that he might determine the factors that had the greatest influence on improvement in writing. A comprehensive and systematic meta-analysis such as Hillocks' allows composition researchers to synthesize findings from a number of sources. The weight of such evidence, scrutinized by rigorous statistical procedures, can be persuasive.

There are, however, a number of problems. Lauer and Asher outline some of the debates over the method, including problems with differences in research designs, variations in the quality of studies, biases depending on the source of the studies (e.g., refereed journals versus dissertations), the time period from which the studies are sampled, and so on. In addition, meta-analysis amplifies all the epistemological problems with positivistic quantitative research. We must subscribe to a view of the world that allows us to define and control variables, treat subjects, and measure effects in quantitative terms in order to place value on these kinds of inquiries.

QUANTITATIVE DESCRIPTIVE STUDIES

Lauer and Asher use the term "quantitative descriptive studies" to describe studies that examine variables with statistical measures (e.g., descriptive statistics such as mean, median, mode, standard deviation, and comparisons such as correlation). They are unlike experimental studies in that they do not compare experimental groups to each other or to control groups, and they do not involve a treatment. This approach was the one most widely used by the process researchers cited earlier. In my own study of revision, for example, I wanted to determine what kinds of revisions students could make in their writing after twelve years of instruction. I identified thousands of revisions in 200 first and second drafts of one assignment, classified them into categories, and used a regression analysis to determine whether certain kinds of revisions were associated with improvements between the first drafts and the second drafts. This kind of approach was typical in the late 1970s and early 1980s as researchers identified features of composing processes and described them quantitatively. (See Lauer and Asher for additional examples and methods.)

The chief advantage of these kinds of studies is that they allow researchers to describe patterns within data or subjects. They can help us to determine, for example, which kinds of revision or invention strategies are being employed most often across a large number of writers. They share some of the disadvantages of experimental studies such as inattention to context and dependence upon controlled conditions. I could not argue, for example, that twelfth graders revised in the same way when they initiated their own writing or when they had more investment in the writing assignment. I could only describe what they did when several hundred of them in a school were asked to write a single kind of paper over several school days. Because they focus on large groups, quantitative descriptive studies reveal little about individual differences unless the researcher embeds case studies within the design.

Qualitative Studies

CASE STUDIES

Case study research has been one of the most popular choices among composition researchers because it allows close observations and insights into the mind of the writer. Janet Emig's case studies of the composing processes of twelfth graders set the tone for dozens that followed. She and a colleague (Emig and Birnbaum) cite Oliver Sacks' book *The Man Who Mistook His Wife for a Hat* in their history of case study research; the nineteenth century, according to Sacks, was a high point for writing "richly clinical tales," and he cites Freud and Luria, among others, as examples of authors of such narratives. While most current case studies in research are narratives or qualitative descriptions, we could easily produce more quantitative case studies (e.g., an analysis of all the textual revisions a student makes over a term).

Emig and Birnbaum (see also Asher and Lauer; Bissex and Bullock; and North for other discussions of case study research) suggest six advantages of case study research, borrowing from the work of Lincoln and Guba. Case study research

1. builds an "emic" reconstruction of the respondents' constructions, in contrast to an "etic" one that would reinforce a positivist's *a priori* inquiries;
2. builds on the interaction between the reader and the research; the narrative is presented as holistic and lifelike descriptions of events, not unlike those the reader would normally experience;
3. exposes the interactions between the inquirer and the respondent (i.e., case study subject);
4. allows the reader to challenge the work by searching for internal consistency, trustworthiness;
5. provides "thick description" or triangulated data (see Geertz), thus improving the likelihood that the reader can see implications for new settings;
6. provides a grounded picture of context.

Other important characteristics of good case study research include careful selection of the subjects so that they will stand as representatives for some larger class and the use of multiple sources of data.

The chief disadvantage, from an experimentalist's point of view, is the lack of generalizability. The events reported about an individual may or may not reflect the patterns that might be found across large groups. The solution to this problem lies in careful selection of the subjects and in careful detail and documentation within the study. Like clinical studies in the health sciences, the advantages lie in the ability to see multiple possibilities for understanding the case. Much responsibility is placed on the reader, who must look for the analogies and differences between the case study and any new contexts where insights from the case study might be relevant. In sharp contrast, little is supposedly left to interpretation in experimental studies. Other problems with case studies also arise when a "clinical" setting for observation is too artificial to have much bearing on writing or composing in more natural surroundings or when practices such as "talk-aloud protocols" color the findings.

ETHNOGRAPHIES

In an extraordinarily helpful overview of ethnography in the language arts, Zaharlick and Green describe ethnography as a "deliberate inquiry process guided by a point of view or cultural theory." They stress that ethnographers must be concerned about how the parts (pieces of a culture) relate to the whole culture, how the differing views, methods, theories, and data interact as the study progresses, and how ethnography fits into the larger context of ethnology, the comparative study of cultures. They provide a useful list of the possible data that ethnographers can collect, such as accounts of everyday events, norms for these events, artifacts, roles, and relationships, particular cultural practices such as schooling and their connections to the social group being studied. They also supply a most helpful outline of necessary features of thorough ethnographies:

1. A complete overview, including the purpose and rationale, a description of the population, a brief summary of the means the ethnographer used to gain access to the group, the roles of the ethnographer, the tools and techniques, the methods of data collection and analysis.
2. A detailed statement about access, including all the negotiations the ethnographer used to gain access to various members of the social group.

3. The role of the ethnographer ("emic" or insider, versus "etic" or observer, outsider).
4. A thorough description of the tools used (e.g., field notes, tapes, photographs, diaries).
5. A complete outline of data collection procedures, including schedules and changes over time.

In composition research, in particular, we might want to add careful analyses of texts, placed in the context of the larger ethnography. The actual narratives in ethnography differ according to the audience, the theoretical premises and style of the ethnographer, and the type of ethnographic study, but Zaharlick and Green recommend Van Maanen's *Tales of the Field: On Writing Ethnography* as a useful source.

The advantages of ethnography over quantitative, large-scale studies, like those for case studies, are due to the ease with which the reader can understand the context and the possible interpretations of the data. Multiple interpretations are possible and encouraged in ethnographies and in case studies. Although multiple interpretations are *possible* in experimental research, they are less likely because the experimentalist's rhetoric is limited to discussions of carefully defined variables. Ethnography introduces larger social and cultural interpretations that may or may not be possible in a narrow case study, particularly if the researcher in a case study limits the field of vision to a few subjects isolated from social interaction. (See also North; Lauer and Asher; Kantor, Kirby, and Goetz; and Calkins for detailed descriptions of ethnographic advantages and methods.)

Lauer and Asher, drawing from Sadler, also offer a list of ten potential pitfalls in naturalistic research (e.g., data overload, availability of information, uneven reliability of information, confusion between cooccurrence and causality). These are important concerns for any ethnographer to address, but they also stem largely from a research paradigm that stresses external truth, leading to the existence of reliability and objectivity. The ethnographer might argue that her or his work exists to challenge such notions and to provide alternative readings of individuals, social groups, and cultures.

TEACHER-RESEARCH
Marian Mohr and Marion Maclean, who describe themselves and many others (see also Goswami and Stillman, Myers) as "teacher-researchers," were among the first to argue for classroom-based, highly con-

textualized research. About their methods, they write: "What teachers have to add to educational research is the sorely missed context of the classroom." Arguing for qualitative, hypothesis-raising, and descriptive methods, they make it clear that "traditional educational research, based on the experimental, hypothesis-testing model with its limited variables, has not always served teachers well" (4). Granted, teachers are not the single or even the primary audience for much academic research on writing; nevertheless, they are an important, and often ignored, set of readers. On the effects of more naturalistic approaches to research on literacy, Louise Phelps comments, "This approach has been so productive and its research so integrated with classroom practice that its theoretical principles are filtering into pedagogy much more rapidly and easily than usual" (114). Her views are also shared by Lucy Calkins, who calls for "research communities among naturalistic researchers."

While Phelps and others might include teacher-research in the category of ethnographic or naturalistic research, Mohr and Maclean are clear that their work has unique benefits and that it is not the same as ethnography: "Teacher-researchers deal with the same participant-observer role tension, but for them the starting point is one of participation, not observation—immersion, not distance. Distance is for teacher-researchers the ultimately unachievable condition, just as participation is for an ethnographer" (55). These advantages for research are clear; the chief disadvantage of teacher-research is that the traditional research community may question the research credentials or the "objectivity" of those they perceive as mainly "practitioners" (North).

General Issues

In composition research, we have clashing epistemologies. They exist within the communities of researchers, and among the consumers of composition research. Most college writing teachers are trained in the humanities and look toward analysis, deductive reasoning, rationalist introspection, and other forms of theoretical speculation more often than they look to experimental, empirical research for answers. Secondary English teachers are trained in colleges of education and are also unlikely to develop sophisticated skills with experimental jargon in their undergraduate programs. Writing teachers deal more in complexities and uncertainties than in probabilities or statistical principles. They tend to prefer classroom narratives over experimental studies. As Stephen North has pointed out, positivist methods of research constitute a "method that seeks to approach certainty by reducing uncertainty." One can never quite apprehend truth with this model of research, but there is never any doubt that truth (in this case, a patterned, systematic theory of "human science") is out there. Many teachers know very well that "It varies" is a better answer than some of the predictive equations derived from statistical models.

So why do we continue to seek answers in quantitative studies?

Even though compositionists are not always trained in the methods of social science research, as Phelps points out (vi), and even though scientific methods may be inappropriate, composition specialists are often called upon to provide this kind of data to administrators who are accustomed to clear and concise presentations. When composition program directors seek funds for such things as new programs in "writing across the curriculum," reduced class sizes, or classrooms filled with expensive computer technology, they are often asked for "research" that demonstrates the "cost-effectiveness" of such expenditures. Administrators typically find numerical data, often pre-test/post-test measures, more compelling than theoretical arguments, naturalistic research, or case studies that provide potential analogies for the proposed activities. North's argument for organizing his book around the characteristics of researchers was that "we" constitute different research communities. Perhaps there is another more important point: the consumers of our research certainly differ from us. When "hard" scientists, social scientists, and leaders of professional programs make decisions about budgets in our institutions, we are pressured to use the "tools of the master" to get the resources we need for our writing programs. However, I find it hard to imagine many natural scientists or social scientists who would be impressed by some of the inappropriate aping of the social sciences that has gone on in composition research.

Granted, there are some areas where quantitative answers are extremely useful to all of us as research consumers. I can recall dozens of times when I have cited research on the scarcity of sustained writing in the nation's secondary schools, or some of my own quantitative research on revision or composing processes with computers. The answers they provide are useful for answering "how" questions: How much writing is happening? How often do students revise? How are writers using computers differently from typewriters or paper and pen?

How much change is there in sentence complexity from the fourth grade to graduate school? However, the more basic interpretive questions have to be dealt with in qualitative terms: Why did these things happen? Why did other things not happen? What are the underlying assumptions that account for *x, y,* and *z*? What kind of cultural blinders am I wearing when I interpret? Are there competing, coexisting explanations for our observations? And so on.

One of the contributors to Moran and Lunsford's book, John Briggs, invokes rhetoric as a cure for the "the swings between extremes of anxiety and euphoria" on the part of researchers with naive hopes for their endeavors. Echoing an essay by Douglas Park, Briggs observes that "an endemic desire among researchers to build theories of rhetoric and composition, apply them directly to pedagogy, and witness the revolutionary perfection of a discipline" has led to this malady. As one of many who had such naive hopes, I can attest that this was the spirit of the times in the 1970s and early 1980s. Our faith in the ultimate perfect-ability of our theories rested on good works. If we worked hard enough to discover rigorous methodologies, most often social scientific, and used them with rich multidisciplinary theories, our findings could lead us to a theory of composition from which sound pedagogy could be derived. Lloyd-Jones says of his early hopes for empirical research, "if it were just better done, we'd have great improvements in the teaching of writing" (202). Of his more recent views, he writes, "we were probably over-optimistic about what *could* be discovered by empirical methods" (202). Like Briggs, Lloyd-Jones argues that the theoretical home for scholarship in writing is still a humanistic edifice built of philosophy, philology, rhetoric, and literature. He writes, "we belong with the humanists, not with the social workers" (207). I would argue that we need both because writing occurs in the kind of world where social workers may be as important as humanists. The economic and political issues associated with writing within the larger culture lend themselves to methods borrowed from political science and from an-thropology as often as from Lloyd-Jones' favorites.

Conclusion

Even with all the epistemological and methodological differences in the field, we have learned a great deal from composition research. We have learned that our ways of composing are not merely straightforward executions of the structure of the final form of a text. We have learned that writers construct complex cognitive representations of their texts in progress, of their audiences, and of their roles as writers. We know a great deal about how successful writers gather material or revise their drafts, and we are learning to pass these strategies on to novice writers. We have learned about the contexts for writing in composition classrooms, in classes "across the curriculum," in business and industry, and in the individual's own private world. We have learned that some things work as we teach writing (e.g., peer groups, revision) and that some things don't (e.g., extensive teaching of grammatical terminology in lieu of writing). We have also learned that writing can be empowering in some lives, and disabling in others, and a few of the reasons why. We have learned all these things from a body of research that is varied, with sometimes incompatible methodologies.

What we need in composition research may not be "better" methods or "the" appropriate research paradigm, but a way of synthesizing information from diverse sources. The ultimate paradigm shift within composition studies may be the loss of belief in the term "paradigm" as a useful metaphor for what we are seeking. Nearly every empirical researcher I have studied over the past two decades, including myself in earlier studies, refers to the need for a model of the composing process, or, with a small concession to complexity, for a model of the composing process*es*. We have heard repeated calls for a more flexible, humanistic approach within our research (Connors, Bizzell, Burton, Voss). Perhaps what we require is not a model at all.

In elementary school, I won an award for a model of a hydrogen atom that I built out of Ping-Pong balls. In graduate school, I won an award for a model of revision that I built out of boxes and arrows. Both of these awards represented state-of-the-art work for me as a researcher in those times, but now they represent antiquated views of the atom and of the processes involved in writing. Perhaps what we need is what Dale Spender has called a theory of "multidimensional reality," a theory that will allow us to pick up different lenses when we need to view things in diverse ways, a way of seeing that makes our biases transparent. With the clarity of hindsight we can see the limitations of our definitions, methodologies, and our goals for research. Perhaps a conception of research that values diverse perspectives will give us the clarity we need to conduct and to use composition research in the next century. This theory of diversity will be as complex as our visions and objects of inquiry.

Notes

1. Three of the major journals read by composition researchers are *Research in the Teaching of English, College Composition and Communication,* and *Written Communication.* Many others publish composition research findings; they are specialized (e.g., *Journal of Advanced Composition, Rhetoric Review, Journal of Basic Writing, Technical Communication, Anthropology and Education Quarterly*) or they serve audiences and topics beyond composition (e.g., *College English, Educational Researcher*). Other helpful sources for research in composition are the *Longman* and *CCCC Bibliography of Composition and Rhetoric,* edited by Erika Lindemann, bibliographies published in *College Composition and Communication,* and helpful articles on bibliography by Scott (1986) and Scott and Castner (1983).

2. These were the years when I chaired the NCTE Standing Committee on Research, which oversees this journal; editors' reports from Judith Langer and Arthur Applebee on these submissions are recorded in the committee's minutes.

Suggested Readings

Beach, Richard, and Lillian S. Bridwell, eds. *New Directions in Composition Research.* New York: Guilford, 1984.

Cooper, Charles, and Lee Odell. *Research on Composing: Points of Departure.* Urbana, IL: NCTE, 1978.

Flood, James, Julie Jensen, Diane Lapp, and James R. Squire, eds. *Handbook of Research on Teaching the English Language Arts.* New York: Macmillan, 1990.

Freedman, Sarah W., A. H. Dyson, Linda Flower, and Wallace Chafe. *Research in Writing: Past, Present, and Future.* Center for the Study of Writing Technical Report No. 1. Berkeley, CA: U of California, 1987.

Hillocks, George, Jr. *Research on Written Communication: New Directions for Teaching.* Urbana, IL: National Conference on Research in English and ERIC, 1986.

Lauer, Janice M., and J. William Asher. *Composition Research: Empirical Designs.* New York: Oxford UP, 1988.

Lindemann, Erika, ed. *Longman Bibliography of Composition and Rhetoric [1984–86].* New York: Longman, 1987–88.

Moran, Michael G., and Ronald F. Lunsford, eds. *Research in Composition and Rhetoric: A Bibliographic Sourcebook.* Westport, CT: Greenwood, 1984.

North, Stephen M. *The Making of Knowledge in Composition: Portrait of an Emerging Field.* Upper Montclair, NJ: Boynton/Cook, 1987.

Phelps, Louise Wetherbee. *Composition as a Human Science: Contributions to the Self-Understanding of a Discipline.* New York: Oxford UP, 1988.

Works Cited

Beach, Richard, and Lillian S. Bridwell, eds. *New Directions in Composition Research.* New York: Guilford, 1984.

Berlin, James A. "Contemporary Composition: The Major Pedagogical Theories." *College English* 44 (1982): 765–77.

Bissex, Glenda, and Richard Bullock, eds. *Seeing for Ourselves: Case-Study Research by Teachers of Writing.* Portsmouth, NH: Boynton/Cook, Heinemann, 1987.

Bizzell, Patricia. "Thomas Kuhn, Scientism, and English Studies." *College English* 40 (1979): 764–71.

Braddock, Richard, Richard Lloyd-Jones, and L. Schoer. *Research in Written Composition.* Champaign, IL: NCTE, 1963.

Bridwell, Lillian S., and Richard Beach. Introduction. *New Directions in Composition Research.* Ed. Richard Beach and Lillian S. Bridwell. New York: Guilford, 1984. 1–14.

Bridwell-Bowles, Lillian S. "Designing Research on Computer-Assisted Writing." *Computers and Composition* 7 (1989): 79–91.

———. "Revising Strategies in Twelfth-Grade Students' Transactional Writing." *Research in the Teaching of English* 14 (1980): 197–222.

Bridwell-Bowles, Lillian S., Parker Johnson, and Stephen Brehe. "Composing and Computers: Case Studies of Experienced Writers." *Writing in Real Time: Modeling Production Processes.* Ed. Ann Matsuhashi. New York: Ablex, 1987. 81–107.

Bridwell-Bowles, Lillian S., Geoffrey Sirc, and Robert Brooke. "Revising and Computing: Case Studies of Student Writers." *The Acquisition of Written Language: Revision and Response.* Ed. Sarah Warshauer Freedman. Norwood, NJ: Ablex, 1985. 172–94.

Briggs, John. "Philosophy and Rhetoric." *Research in Composition and Rhetoric: A Bibliographic Sourcebook.* Ed. Michael G. Moran and Ronald F. Lunsford. Westport, CT: Greenwood, 1984. 93–124.

Burton, Dwight L. "Research in the Teaching of English: The Troubled Dream." *Research in the Teaching of English* 7 (1973): 160–89.

Burton, Fredrick R. "Teacher-Researcher Projects: An Elementary School Teacher's Perspective." *Handbook of Research on Teaching the English Language Arts.* Ed. James Flood et al. New York: Macmillan, 1990.

Calkins, Lucy M. "Forming Research Communities among Naturalistic Researchers." *Perspectives on Research and Scholarship in Composition.* Ed. Ben McClelland and Timothy Donovan. New York: MLA, 1985. 125–44.

Connors, Robert J. "Composition Studies and Science." *College English* 45 (1983): 1–20.

———. "The Rise and Fall of the Modes of Discourse." *College Composition and Communication* 32 (1981): 444–63.

Cooper, Charles, and Lee Odell. *Research on Composing: Points of Departure.* Urbana, IL: NCTE, 1978.

Coulthard, Malcolm. *An Introduction to Discourse Analysis.* London: Longman, 1977.

Culler, Jonathan. *On Deconstruction: Theory and Criticism after Structuralism.* Ithaca: Cornell UP, 1982.

Deising, Paul. *Patterns of Discovery in the Social Sciences.* New York: Aldine, 1971.

Dobrin, David N. "Protocols Once More." *College English* 48 (1986): 713–25.

Emig, Janet. *The Composing Processes of Twelfth Graders.* Research Report No. 13. Champaign, IL: NCTE, 1971. ERIC ED 058 205.

Emig, Janet, and June Birnbaum. "Case Study." *Handbook of Research on Teaching the English Language Arts.* Ed. James Flood et al. New York: Macmillan, 1990.

Flood, James, Julie Jensen, Diane Lapp, and James R. Squire, eds. *Handbook of Research on Teaching the English Language Arts.* New York: Macmillan, 1990.

Flower, Linda, and John R. Hayes. "A Cognitive Process Theory of Writing." *College Composition and Communication* 32 (1981): 365–87.

Freedman, Sarah W., A. H. Dyson, Linda Flower, and Wallace Chafe. *Research in Writing: Past, Present, and Future.* Center for the Study of Writing Technical Report No. 1. Berkeley: U of California, 1987.

Geertz, Clifford. *The Interpretation of Cultures.* New York: Basic Books, 1973.

Goswami, Dixie, and Peter Stillman, eds. *Reclaiming the Classroom: Teacher-Research as an Agency for Change.* Portsmouth, NH: Boynton/Cook, Heinemann, 1987.

Herrington, Anne J. "The First Twenty Years of Research in the Teaching of English and the Growth of a Research Community in Composition Studies." *Research in the Teaching of English* 23 (1989): 117–38.

Hillocks, George, Jr. *Research on Written Communication: New Directions for Teaching.* Urbana, IL: National Conference on Research in English and ERIC, 1986.

————. "What Works in Teaching Composition: A Meta-Analysis of Experimental Treatment Studies." *American Journal of Education* 93 (1984): 133–70.

Hoyt, F. S. "Grammar in the Elementary Curriculum." *Teachers College Record* 8 (1906): 467–500.

Kantor, Kenneth J., Dan R. Kirby, and Judith P. Goetz. "Research in Context: Ethnographic Studies in English." *Research in the Teaching of English* 15 (1981): 293–310.

King, Martha L. "Research in Composition: A Need for Theory." *Research in the Teaching of English* 2 (1978): 193–202.

Kleine, Michael. "Syntactic Choice and a Theory of Discourse: Rethinking Sentence-Combining." Diss. U of Minnesota, 1983.

Lauer, Janice M., and J. William Asher. *Composition Research: Empirical Designs*. New York: Oxford UP, 1988.

Lincoln, Yvonna S., and Egon G. Guba. *Naturalistic Inquiry*. Beverly Hills, CA: Sage, 1985.

Lindemann, Erika, ed. *Longman Bibliography of Composition and Rhetoric, 1984–1985*. New York: Longman, 1987.

————. *Longman Bibliography of Composition and Rhetoric, 1986*. New York: Longman, 1988.

Lloyd-Jones, Richard. "What We May Become." *College Composition and Communication* 33 (1982): 202–07.

Lyman, Rollo L. *Summary of Investigations Relating to Grammar, Language, and Composition*. Chicago: U of Chicago P, 1929.

Matsuhashi, Anne. "Pausing and Planning: The Tempo of Written Discourse Production." *Research in the Teaching of English* 15 (1981): 113–34.

McLaren, Peter. "Critical Literacy and the Postmodern Turn: Cautions from the Margins." Paper presented at the Multidisciplinary Perspectives on Literacy Research Conference, NCTE Assembly on Research, Chicago, 1990.

Mohr, Marian M., and Marion S. Maclean. *Working Together: A Guide for Teacher-Researchers*. Urbana, IL: NCTE, 1987.

Moran, Michael G., and Ronald F. Lunsford, eds. *Research in Composition and Rhetoric: A Bibliographic Sourcebook*. Westport, CT: Greenwood, 1984.

Myers, Miles. "A Model for the Composing Process." National Writing Project Occasional Paper No. 3. Berkeley: U of California-Berkeley, 1980.

————. *The Teacher-Researcher: How to Study Writing in the Classroom*. Urbana, IL: NCTE, 1985.

North, Stephen M. *The Making of Knowledge in Composition: Portrait of an Emerging Field*. Upper Montclair, NJ: Boynton/Cook, 1987.

O'Donnell, Roy C. "Theory, Research, and Practice in Teaching the English

Language Arts." *Handbook of Research on Teaching the English Language Arts.* Ed. James Flood et al. New York: Macmillan, 1990.

Phelps, Louise Wetherbee. *Composition as a Human Science: Contributions to the Self-Understanding of a Discipline.* New York: Oxford UP, 1988.

Sadler, D. R. "Intuitive Data Processing as a Potential Source of Bias in Naturalistic Evaluations." *Educational Evaluation and Policy Analysis* 3 (1981): 25–31.

Scott, Patrick. "Bibliographical Problems in Research on Composition." *College Composition and Communication* 37 (1986): 167–77.

Scott, Patrick, and Bruce Castner. "Reference Sources for Composition Research: A Practical Survey." *College English* 45 (1983): 756–68.

Smith, Carl B., and Susan S. Klein. "Syntheses of Research in Language Arts Instruction." *Handbook of Research on Teaching the English Language Arts.* Ed. James Flood et al. New York: Macmillan, 1990.

Spender, Dale. *Man Made Language.* 2nd ed. London: Routledge & Kegan Paul, 1985.

Steinberg, Erwin R. "Protocols, Retrospective Reports, and the Stream of Consciousness." *College English* 48 (1986): 697–712.

Stotsky, Sandra, and Cindy Mall. "Understanding Research on Teaching the English Language Arts: An Introduction." *Handbook of Research on Teaching the English Language Arts.* Ed. James Flood et al. New York: Macmillan, 1990.

van Dijk, Teun A. *Text and Context: Explorations in the Semantics and Pragmatics of Discourse.* London: Longman, 1977.

Van Maanen, J. *Tales of the Field: On Writing Ethnography.* Chicago: U of Chicago P, 1988.

Voss, Ralph F. "Composition and the Empirical Imperative." *Journal of Advanced Composition* 4 (1983): 5–11.

White, Edward M. *Teaching and Assessing Writing.* San Francisco: Jossey-Bass, 1986.

Zaharlick, Amy, and Judith L. Green. "Ethnographic Research." *Handbook of Research on Teaching the English Language Arts.* Ed. James Flood et al. New York: Macmillan, 1990.

Teaching Writing

Lisa Ede

OREGON STATE UNIVERSITY

In an often-quoted passage in *Language as Symbolic Action,* Kenneth Burke notes that: "Even if any given terminology is a *reflection* of reality, by its very nature as a terminology it must be a *selection* of reality; and to this extent it must function also as a *deflection* of reality" (45). Although Burke is here speaking specifically about language, his comments remind us more generally that the way in which we direct our attention in part determines what we perceive. This is certainly true of the teaching of writing.

If we examine the material conditions that characterize the teaching of writing in North America today, for instance, we see a disturbing picture, one described in the Conference on College Composition and Communication's 1989 *Statement of Principles and Standards for the Postsecondary Teaching of Writing:*

> More than half of the English faculty in two-year colleges, and nearly one-third of the English faculty at four-year colleges and universities, work on part-time and/or temporary appointments. Almost universally, they are teachers of writing. . . . These teachers work without job security, often without benefits, and for wages far below what their full-time colleagues are paid per course. Increasingly, many are forced to accept an itinerant existence, racing from class to car to drive to another institution to teach. (330)

If we narrow our focus to one aspect of this overcrowded scene, the textbooks used by the often overworked and underprepared instructors who teach the majority of composition classes, the picture becomes only a shade less bleak. For as Donald Stewart notes in a review of recent composition textbooks, despite the presence of a number of innovative ones, many commercially successful textbooks continue to present traditional formulas and models. Because underprepared and overworked teachers often rely upon textbooks to structure most in- and out-of-class activities, textbooks mirror an important reality about the teaching of writing.

By shifting our gaze, we can compose a more optimistic portrait. The development of composition studies as a field—the growth of graduate programs and of journals, conferences, and other scholarly apparatus—has inevitably influenced the teaching of writing. The faculty member directing a writing program is now likely to be someone with a Ph.D. in composition studies, someone who actually wants and is trained to do the job. These and other developments in the field must be seen as positive, but they cannot obviate the fact that there continues to be a substantial gap between what researchers and experienced practitioners in the field know about the teaching of writing and how writing is actually taught in many community colleges, colleges, and universities.

Any discussion of the teaching of writing must begin by acknowledging this situation. Furthermore, this acknowledgment compels us to recognize that research on writing can have only limited impact on the actual *teaching* of writing as long as current conditions persist. Teachers of writing must work together to challenge such inequitable and pedagogically inappropriate practices as the exploitation of part-time instructors. While doing so we must also, of course, continue to teach our courses—to make decisions about textbooks, assignments, grading, and other classroom matters.

Teachers attempting to make informed decisions about matters such as these face a number of difficulties. One involves the sheer volume of research on writing. As the review that I undertook before beginning this essay reminded me, over the past twenty-five years we have amassed a considerable body of theoretical, historical, pedagogical, quantitative, and qualitative research on the teaching of writing. Each of us can name efforts that have had a significant impact on our field. My own list includes studies of the composing process, of invention and revision, of the relationship of cognitive development and writing, of basic writing, of the role of audience in discourse, of the impact of computers on writing, of assessment, of the writing-reading relationship, of style, of collaborative learning and writing, of rhetorical theory, and of the history of writing instruction.

This list, incomplete as it is, is impressive. But reading research on the teaching of writing may not resolve teachers' problems. Indeed, as teaching assistants taking their first composition theory class often attest, it can (at least in the short term) exacerbate them. For how, teaching assistants often ask in frustration, should they apply the knowledge they're gaining in the classes they teach? And what are they to make of the many conflicts that characterize the field of composition studies? For these and other writing teachers the often-asked question "What do we *know* about the teaching of writing?" may not be as crucial as another question: "What can and should teachers *do* with what we know about the teaching of writing?"

Some theorists have responded to this question by attempting to categorize various approaches to the teaching of writing. By grouping assumptions and practices into coherent "approaches," theorists such as James Berlin, Lester Faigley, Richard Fulkerson, Paul Kameen, and Richard Young hope, in Berlin's terms, to help "writing teachers become more aware of the full significance of their pedagogical strategies" ("Contemporary Composition" 766). Like Berlin, in this essay I hope to help writing teachers become more theoretically sophisticated and more confident practitioners. Rather than surveying various approaches to the teaching of writing, however, I will follow a different strategy. I will suggest what might best be thought of as a way of reading the diverse and constantly growing body of research on the teaching of writing and of thinking about the relationship of theory and practice. For although approaches to the teaching of writing can be described and grouped, although experts have written and will continue to write books about what we "know" about the teaching of writing, composition teachers will always have to negotiate a minefield of competing theories and research studies, just as they will always have to evaluate the consequences of these efforts for their practice.

Woven throughout my discussion are a number of references to the work of Peter Elbow. I have chosen to focus on Elbow not because he is a major theorist of composition—although he is—or because I wish to attack or defend his views. Rather, Elbow's work is helpful for my purposes because, for a variety of reasons, it has attracted both strong proponents and equally strong attackers and thus represents the sort of "problem" that teachers of writing attempting to evaluate authoritative knowledge for pedagogical practices regularly face.

Consider, for instance, the case of freewriting. Freewriting, is, as most teachers of writing know, a method identified with Ken Macrorie and Peter Elbow; here I will be concerned with Elbow's advocacy of freewriting. From the start, Elbow has made strong claims for freewriting. *Writing Without Teachers,* published in 1974, begins with this sentence: "The most effective way I know to improve your writing is to do freewriting exercises regularly" (3). Eight years later—years during which considerable research on the teaching of writing in general and on invention in particular was published—Elbow makes similar claims in *Writing with Power: Techniques for Mastering the Writing Process:* "Freewriting is the easiest way to get words on paper and the best all around practice in writing that I know" (13).

Elbow's claims have been affirmed in a variety of ways. Elbow's books and essays have influenced a whole generation of teachers. A 1989 survey of ninth-grade English teachers in the Corvallis, Oregon, school district, for instance, indicated that more teachers were familiar with Elbow's work than with that of any other theorist (Howry). Most composition textbooks include freewriting as an inventional strategy. And recently freewriting has attracted traditional scholarly analysis as well. In *Nothing Begins with N: New Investigations of Freewriting,* Pat Belanoff, Peter Elbow, and Sheryl Fontaine present a number of discussions of freewriting, including case and experimental studies of the effects of freewriting on students.

But freewriting has also met with criticism. Perhaps the strongest attack has come from George Hillocks' *Research on Written Composition: New Directions for Teaching,* the 1986 study that evaluates empirical research on composition published from 1963, the year of Richard Braddock, Richard Lloyd-Jones, and Lowell Schoer's *Research in Written Composition,* to 1982. This study, which uses the statistical process of meta-analysis, ends with recommendations for teachers of writing. Freewriting does not fare well in this analysis.

Hillocks begins his discussion of freewriting by noting that "research on the composing process [Hillocks here refers to a wide variety of studies, many of which were not included in his meta-analysis] provides little evidence to suggest that free writing as a main focus . . . of instruction will be effective" (231). Hillocks goes on to report that his meta-analysis confirms this inference: freewriting, Hillocks states, "has only minimal effect on the quality of writing" (232). Later, in discussing what he terms the "foci of instruction," Hillocks comments that "as a major instructional technique, free writing is more effective than teaching grammar [the least effective focus of instruction studied] in raising the quality of student writing. However, it is less effective than any other focus of instruction examined" (249).

Set in stark opposition, Elbow's and Hillocks' emphatically contradictory claims about freewriting are so unsettling that it is tempting to bracket them, to dismiss them as atypical. But in fact many similar contradictions abound in discussions of the teaching of writing. Consider, for instance, arguments about the use of heuristics. In the early 1970s, Janice Lauer and Ann E. Berthoff debated the value of heuristics in the pages of *College Composition and Communication*. Lauer (1970) asserted that heuristic procedures developed by psychologists have much to offer theorists and teachers of writing. Berthoff responded by charging that such methods are "philosophically disastrous and politically dangerous" (95).

Or consider arguments about the best way to help students learn to revise. "Can you teach revision through specific writing tasks?" John Warnock asks in "The Writing Process": "Hillocks said yes. [Donald] Murray said no" (10). These debates point to a larger issue, the proper role that teachers of writing should play when they work with students. As Lil Brannon observes, some teachers—Brannon calls them "transmission" teachers—"believe that teachers can give writers skills and strategies" (22). Brannon includes in this group such researchers as Richard Young, Frank D'Angelo, and Linda Flower. Others, whom Brannon calls "reactive" teachers, "emphasize encouraging writers to use the latent resources they already have" (23). Donald Murray, Peter Elbow, and William E. Coles, Jr., are notable members of this group.

What is at least partly at stake in this debate, of course, is the question of whether writing can be taught or only assisted, supported, encouraged. Often playing a hidden role in this opposition are other issues. As Sylvia Scribner and Michael Cole point out, for instance, "In practice, a prototypical form of text [such as the personal narrative essay or technical report] underlies most analyses of the writing process" (60). Some writers recognize this inevitable bias. In the first chapter of *Problem-Solving Strategies for Writing,* for example, Linda Flower notes that her textbook focuses on "the problems people face when they need to write academic papers, persuasive reports, concise memos, and essays that can open a reader's eyes" (1). Other theorists and textbook writers are less explicit about the prototypical genres or forms of text that their discussions of writing and of the writing process assume.

We should not be surprised that Flower's prototypical text differs from that of, say Murray or Coles. The single term "writing" can never cover or evoke all the various uses we actually make of writing in our

lives—from jotting down grocery lists to writing letters and journals
and composing legal briefs and technical reports. As Warnock notes:
"Though 'writing' is often used with an apparent confidence that we all
know what we mean by the term, that confidence is as unwarranted as
our sometime confidence about the term 'literacy' " (3).

Metaphor also plays an important role in discussions of writing, for
we can never have complete or unmediated access to the process of
writing. David Bartholomae and Anthony Petrosky acknowledge this
reliance on metaphor in *Facts, Artifacts, and Counterfacts: Theory and
Method for a Reading and Writing Course* when they introduce their
study by noting that "This book is not only a description of the [Univer-
sity of Pittsburgh's basic writing] course as we are teaching it now, but it
is also an extended presentation of the metaphors we have chosen to
represent our subject" (4). (Bartholomae and Petrosky note, for instance, that "we choose to represent our student readers as composers
rather than decoders" [15].) Linda Flower and John R. Hayes make a
similar observation at the start of "The Cognition of Discovery: Defining a Rhetorical Problem": "Metaphors give shape to mysteries, and
traditionally we have used the metaphor of *discovery* to describe the
writer's creative process" (22).

Even when theorists such as Flower and Hayes and Bartholomae and
Petrosky attempt to acknowledge the metaphors that animate their vision of writing and the writing process, much inevitably remains hidden, unexplored. In "Control in Writing: Flower, Derrida, and Images
of the Writer," Robert Brooke deconstructs Flower and her colleagues'
work to demonstrate the role that the unacknowledged metaphor of
"control" plays in Flower's texts: "the explicit rhetorical purpose of her
texts is to help teachers and students 'control' their writing processes,
yet the processes she describes are dynamically *beyond* control" (407).
Brooke's Derridean reading of Flower causes him to propose that teachers of writing should help students "accept a different way of imagining
themselves—a way of conceiving of the self which is not as threatened
or troubled by internal confusion as the seemingly commonsensical
classical subject" (416).

This discussion of metaphor leads us back to Elbow's and Hillocks'
conflicting claims about freewriting. Elbow's books abound with metaphors; metaphors also play a crucial role in Elbow's argument. *Writing
with Power* utilizes what Elbow calls the "cookbook strategy" of giving
readers a variety of techniques for particular purposes, such as getting

feedback or generating ideas. Like a writer of a cookbook, Elbow thus "provide[s] choice . . . but within any given recipe I have not hesitated to spell out in explicit detail the steps you should follow" (8). As might be expected, Hillocks' use of metaphor differs sharply from that of Elbow. *Research on Written Communication* generally avoids the use of obvious metaphors, though it cannot entirely do so. Hillocks' favored mode of instruction, the "environmental" mode, for instance, depends not only on the results of meta-analysis but also on the metaphoric implications of the term "environmental" for its persuasive impact.

A critical reading of the acknowledged and unacknowledged metaphors that inform both Elbow's and Hillocks' work might provide a way to get beyond or beneath their disagreement about freewriting to more foundational issues. For as Phillip K. Arrington notes in "Tropes of the Composing Process," tropes, such as metaphor, have the capacity "to prefigure our ideological stances toward language and writing" (335) and thus open up new space for discussion. In "Modernism and the Scene(s) of Writing," for instance, Linda Brodkey demonstrates how the suppressed metaphor of the scene of writing—that of "a solitary writer alone in a garret working into the small hours of the morning" (396)—has influenced the teaching of writing. Brodkey urges us to reexamine our thinking about writers and writing; to do so, we must "begin not by ignoring the scene of writing, but by reinserting some of the tensions between readers, writers, and texts that the world represented in the scene of writing so artfully supresses" (397).

Tropological/rhetorical/ideological analysis (choose your term) such as Arrington's and Brodkey's holds great promise, for it provides a potential way to critique apparently oppositional claims such as those of Hillocks and Elbow regarding freewriting. A reading of these authors' works might ask questions such as these. What makes freewriting "free"? What is the nature of the "analysis" that grounds and guarantees the accuracy of Hillocks' meta-analysis? What, in other words, do Elbow and Hillocks assume as a common-sense grounding for their pedagogical advice? What presence operates, in Derridean terms, to make their approaches appear coherent and unassailable?

Until we see beyond these deferring claims to more central issues, until we are able, in Brodkey's terms, to reinsert some of the tensions that Elbow's and Hillocks' texts inevitably suppress, their disagreement remains a problem—rather than a fruitfully problematized site for exploration. What can or should teaching assistants taking a composition theory class "do," for instance, with Elbow's and Hillocks' contrasting assertions about freewriting? Must they choose between one or the other "camp"? Some students will approach these works with such strong predispositions that they will automatically do so. Others will grant that, despite these authors' disagreement about freewriting, both may be if not right then useful. Such students will thus pick and choose those aspects of Elbow's and Hillocks' work that seem helpful or effective given their own teaching style, situation, and students.

Both of these strategies have the virtue of maintaining collegiality—a virtue not lost on teaching assistants struggling to understand and survive academic politics. In some writing programs, adherents of Elbow and Hillocks can teach different sections of the same freshman composition course and not even know that they disagree about fundamental issues, while those who pick and choose from both can offend no one. In this regard, composition teachers have proven no different from English teachers in general who, as Gerald Graff points out in *Professing Literature: An Institutional History,* have tended to operate "on a principle of systematic non-relationship in which all parties tacitly agree not to ask how they might be connected or opposed" (8–9).

Writing of this situation in "Peace Plan for the Canon Wars," Gerald Graff and William E. Cain argue that the solution to theoretical and pedagogical conflicts should be neither "pluralistic evasion" (312) nor forced agreement. Rather, they argue that English teachers should instead "teach the conflicts" (312). In the case of composition studies, this means recognizing that teachers of writing need to address, not evade, the question of how we can best evaluate authoritative knowledge for pedagogical practices in composition. Considered in this light, Elbow's and Hillocks' disagreement about the pedagogical usefulness of freewriting is finally not a problem but rather an opportunity.

If we accept Graff and Cain's challenge to confront, rather than evade, theoretical and pedagogical differences in the teaching of writing, we will have to give up one of our favorite accommodational strategies: our hasty retreat when challenged to the assertion that a particular pedagogical approach or practice "works best for me and my students." Rejecting this strategy does not mean, however, that teachers of writing should ignore the specifics of their classroom and institution. Whatever the subject or level, teaching is, as my colleague Suzanne Clark eloquently affirms, "a rhetorical act, a language art." Accordingly, teachers—like all who use language—must be sensitive to their rhetorical situations. But just as sensitivity to a writer's rhetorical situation involves much more than considering demographic information about the writer's audience, so too does sensitivity to a teacher's rhetorical situation involve more than simple observation and adaptation. For rhetoric has always recognized—though it has not always used these terms—that "the self is already within ideology and language" (Jarratt and Grogan 5).

As teachers probe and clarify their rhetorical situations, they need to recognize the cultural, political, and ideological forces influencing both them and their students. They also need to establish a heuristic, dialectical relationship between theory and practice. Theory should inform practice, certainly—but practice must also inform theory, for practice also (we too easily forget) is knowledge-generating. And what is practice but the interaction of specific teachers and students in specific situations, the moment-to-moment rhetorical reality of the classroom?

Despite increasingly strong arguments for writing as a social process (Brodkey, Cooper, Gere, Reither, and Vipond), composition theorists have only recently begun to probe the significance of students' and teachers' rhetorical situations. Much attention has been focused, for instance, on arguments for a social constructionist epistemology (Berlin, Bruffee, Le Fevre, Reither). As Joseph Harris notes in "The Idea of Community in the Study of Writing," however, these arguments often ignore powerful cultural, political, and ideological aspects of students' situations. Thus, Harris argues, theorists have erred in treating the concept of discourse community as a monolithic construct, forgetting that students—and teachers—are "always *simultaneously* a part of several discourses, of several communities . . . [are] always already committed to a number of conflicting practices" (19).

Similarly, in "Collaboration, Resistance, and the Teaching of Writing," Suzanne Clark and I argue that advocates of social constructionist theories, such as Bruffee, have overlooked the significance of resistance for theory and practice. Discussion of this concept must, we believe, be grounded in an analysis of the rhetorical situation of the classroom. Such analysis "complicates and enriches our understanding of resistance because it reminds us that teachers must always contend with the authority that their position constructs; students must always deal with their lack of authority" (12).

As the above examples demonstrate, the failure adequately to consider teachers' and students' rhetorical situations has potentially significant implications for research in composition studies. Consider, for instance, James A. Berlin's discussion of Elbow in *Rhetoric and Reality: Writing Instruction in American Colleges, 1900–1985*. In this well-known work, Berlin uses epistemology as the basis for his critique of various approaches to the teaching of writing:

> Objective theories locate reality in the external world, in the material objects of experience. Subjective theories place truth within the subject, to be discovered through an act of internal apprehension. And transactional theories [which Berlin subdivides into classical, cognitive, and epistemic theories] locate reality at the point of interaction of subject and object, with audience and language as mediating agencies. (6)

By focusing on epistemological assumptions, Berlin raises crucial theoretical issues and effectively highlights the way in which "in teaching writing we are providing students with guidance in seeing and structuring their experience, with a set of tacit rules about distinguishing truth from falsity, reality from illusion" (7). But this emphasis also causes Berlin to privilege some issues and practices while ignoring or devaluing others.

By privileging epistemology, for instance, Berlin deemphasizes the consequences of Elbow's commitment to writing groups. Berlin argues that Elbow's approach must be classified as subjective rather than epistemic—Berlin's favored category—because his "commitment to an epistemology that locates all truth within a personal construct arising from one's unique selfhood . . . prevents . . . [him] from becoming genuinely epistemic in . . . [his] approach, despite . . . [his] use of activities—such as the editorial group—that on the surface are social in nature" (153). But can Elbow's advocacy of writing groups be so easily dismissed? Doesn't this argument ignore the fact that, as Brian Street asserts in *Literacy in Theory and Practice*, "the *processes* whereby reading and writing are learnt are what construct the meaning of it for particular practitioners" (8, my emphasis)?

Patricia Bizzell echoes Street's assertion in "Arguing About Literacy" when she notes that the teaching of writing might best be viewed as the "process of constructing academic literacy, creating it anew in each class through the interaction of the professor's and the students' cultural resources" (150). In her essay, Bizzell comments that although teaching and learning writing—the production of literacy—are inherently collaborative, students and professors are hardly equal partners in this joint venture: "The professor automatically has more persuasive power for what he or she wants to include in academic literacy, simply by virtue of the social power his or her position provides over the students" (150).

Street's and Bizzell's comments suggest that a contextualized, rhetorically and ideologically grounded analysis of Elbow's approach to the teaching of writing must consider not only his epistemological assumptions but such factors as the teacher-student relationship his approach fosters and the kinds of activities that actually occur in writing classes. Such a perspective makes it much less easy to categorize Elbow's work. If teachers and students who employ Elbow's approach not only freewrite and keep journals but also spend considerable class time in group work, can the significance of this activity for the social construction of literacy in the classroom be so easily dismissed? Similarly, don't Elbow's statements about writing—statements that are, as Berlin rightly observes, grounded in the discourse of individualism—need to be examined not just in theory but in the context of actual classroom situations? When Elbow tells students that "everyone can, under certain conditions, speak with clarity and power" (*Power* 7) or that "I am talking to that person inside everyone who has ever written or tried to write . . . who seeks power in words" (*Power* 6), might not these statements represent a wise (if intuitive and thus untheorized) effort to mitigate the inevitable power imbalance between students and teacher that Bizzell describes?

Berlin's analysis of Elbow demonstrates how difficult it is fully to contextualize discussions of the teaching of writing. In *Rhetoric and Reality,* Berlin characterizes transactional theories of rhetoric as "based on an epistemology that sees truth as arising out of the interaction of the elements of the rhetorical situation" (15). Despite this recognition, Berlin himself fails adequately to ground his discussion of Elbow in a fully contextualized consideration of the actual classroom practices Elbow advocates and the way in which those practices may respond to the ideological and political situations of students and teachers. In so doing, Berlin may create an opposition between subjective and social-epistemic rhetoric that exists more strongly in theory than in practice.

My earlier discussion of freewriting attempted to explore the nature of the claims made for and against freewriting, rather than to assess this method. Similarly, this critique of Berlin's discussion of Elbow's work should be read as an exploration of the difficulties involved in *any* effort to analyze the teaching of writing, rather than as an attack upon Berlin or a defense of Elbow. Theorists must establish criteria for analysis; my discussion of Berlin simply confirms Burke's observation that any terminology not only reflects but selects and deflects reality.

My analysis does suggest, however, that current efforts to argue for writing as a social process may rely upon unnecessary and unhelpful oppositions. Furthermore, even though advocates of writing as a social process argue that literacy instruction is embedded in ideology, culture, and politics, this argument does not in itself guarantee that analyses of the teaching of writing grounded in this approach will themselves adequately address these issues. Nor, as Reither and Vipond observe, is there any guarantee that accepting this theoretical position will catalyze changes in actual classroom practices:

> The topic of writing as social process has been a hot one in the last few years, so much so that it has become a dominant strand in our literature and at our conferences. The result has been a kind of revolution in composition theory. Unfortunately, however, the revolution seems to have been confined pretty much to the literature. Although the case for writing's social dimensions no longer requires arguing—it can be assumed—we would be hard put to point to a corresponding transformation in the ways writing is conceived and dealt with in our classrooms. In fact, even though radical changes in practice seem called for if we believe even some of what has been claimed about the social dimensions of writing, little substantive change in either course design or classroom practice has come about that can be said to result directly from this reconsideration of the nature of writing. (855)

Knowing that writing is a social process does not necessarily empower teachers—or students—effectively to resist the structures and discourse of contemporary education.

Reither and Vipond's comments bring us back to the relationship of theory and practice in the teaching of writing, reminding us that theoretical revolutions may—or may not—have significant pedagogical consequences. And perhaps we are distanced enough from the writing-as-process revolution to recognize that this movement, enthusiastically received by college and university writing teachers in the early 1970s but only now filtering down to the public schools, may not have dramatically changed teaching practices. Instead, some teachers of writing may have replaced one narrow and rigid set of practices for another. Teachers who in pre-revolutionary days assured their students that they couldn't possibly compose an effective essay without writing a formal outline before drafting may now require their students to complete a series of prescribed heuristic activities instead.

Despite the large and diverse body of research on the teaching of writing, we are just beginning to recognize the difficult questions raised by a rigorous examination of the relationship of theory and practice. (Louise Wetherbee Phelps makes a useful contribution to discussion of this issue in the final chapter of *Composition as a Human Science: Contributions to the Self-Understanding of a Discipline.*) We have accumulated a large body of information on the teaching of writing in the last twenty-five years, but we are just beginning to explore the reasons why this research has had so little impact on actual practice. We are also just beginning to recognize the extraordinary complexity of these activities that we call writing and teaching, to consider what it means for us *as teachers* when we recognize that all language use, including our own, is embedded in ideology, culture, and politics.

Research in literacy studies offers perhaps the most fruitful grounding for efforts to respond to these and other issues and problems. For when we view writing in the context of literacy studies we are reminded that writing engages students—and teachers—who have not only minds but also bodies and emotions, who bring to school not only their own experiences, interests, desires, and prejudices but also those of their families, neighbors, and community. An ethnographic study like Heath's *Ways with Words: Language, Life, and Work in Communities and Classrooms* forces us to confront how little we know about the "living, believing, and valuing" that our students bring with them to school and how crucial these will be as they attempt to acquire "knowledge and skill in the symbolic manipulation of language" (367).

Heath's study also reminds us that even innovative and effective pedagogical practices, like those Heath developed with local teachers, parents, and students in the Piedmont Carolinas, may not be able to resist larger forces. In the epilogue to *Ways with Words,* Heath notes that thanks to "a decrease in the autonomy of teachers as competent professionals and an increase in the bureaucratization of teaching and testing," the ethnographic methods that teachers had successfully used in the 1970s and that teachers interviewed in 1981 recalled as "a creative high point in their careers" have "all but disappeared" (356).

Although few theorists in literacy studies use the term "rhetorical situation" or see their work grounded in rhetoric, their emphasis on context, ideology, and politics points in the same direction and carries similar implications. When Street argues that "literacy can only be known to us in forms which already have political and ideological significance and it cannot, therefore, be helpfully separated from that significance and treated as if it were an 'autonomous' thing" (8) or when Heath affirms that "the school is not a neutral objective arena; it is an institution which has the goal of changing people's values, skills, and knowledge bases" (367), they are urging us to attend to our and our students' rhetorical situations—though they would not use this term. They are urging us to realize, as Bizzell observes in "Arguing About Literacy," that when we teach writing we are seeking "to persuade a particular audience, in a particular time and place" (148). Such a recognition can raise uncomfortable questions for teachers of writing, for we have tended to evade, rather than to confront, the politically and ideologically situated nature of our work. But though these questions may challenge some of our assumptions and practices, they can also help us remember the vital link between inquiry and action.

Acknowledgments

I would like to thank Chris Anderson, Suzanne Clark, Peter Elbow, Cheryl Glenn, Andrea Lunsford, and Lex Runciman, who responded to earlier drafts of this essay.

Suggested Readings

Bartholomae, David, and Anthony Petrosky. *Facts, Artifacts and Counterfacts: Theory and Method for a Reading and Writing Course.* Upper Montclair, NJ: Boynton/Cook, Heinemann, 1986.

Berlin, James A. *Rhetoric and Reality: Writing Instruction in American Colleges, 1900–1985.* Carbondale: Southern Illinois UP, 1987.

Elbow, Peter. *Writing with Power: Techniques for Mastering the Writing Process.* New York: Oxford UP, 1981.

Enos, Theresa, ed. *A Sourcebook for Basic Writing Teachers.* New York: Random House, 1987.

Hillocks, George, Jr. *Research on Written Composition: New Directions for Teaching.* Urbana, IL: National Conference on Research in English and ERIC, 1986.

Kintgen, Eugene R., Barry M. Kroll, and Mike Rose, eds. *Perspectives on Literacy.* Carbondale: Southern Illinois UP, 1988.

Lindemann, Erika. *A Rhetoric for Writing Teachers.* 2nd ed. New York: Oxford UP, 1987.

Shaughnessy, Mina P. *Errors and Expectations: A Guide for the Teacher of Basic Writing.* New York: Oxford UP, 1977.

Tate, Gary, ed. *Teaching Composition: Twelve Bibliographical Essays.* Fort Worth: Texas Christian UP, 1987.

White, Edward M. *Developing Successful College Writing Programs.* San Francisco: Jossey-Bass, 1989.

Works Cited

Arrington, Philip K. "Tropes of the Composing Process." *College English* 48 (1986): 325–38.

Belanoff, Pat, Peter Elbow, and Sheryl Fontaine, eds. *Nothing Begins with N: New Investigations of Freewriting.* Carbondale: Southern Illinois UP, 1991.

Bartholomae, David, and Anthony Petrosky. *Facts, Artifacts and Counterfacts: Theory and Method for a Reading and Writing Course.* Portsmouth, NH: Boynton/Cook, Heinemann, 1986.

Berlin, James A. "Contemporary Composition: The Major Pedagogical Theories." *College English* 44 (1982): 765–77.

———. "Rhetoric and Ideology in the Writing Class." *College English* 50 (1988): 477–94.

Berthoff, Ann E. "The Problem of Problem-Solving." *Contemporary Rhetoric: A Conceptual Background with Readings.* Ed. W. Ross Winterowd. New York: Harcourt, 1975. 90–96.

Bizzell, Patricia. "Arguing about Literacy." *College English* 50 (1988): 141–53.

Braddock, Richard, Richard Lloyd-Jones, and Lowell Schoer, eds. *Research in Written Composition.* Urbana, IL: NCTE, 1963.

Brannon, Lil. "Toward a Theory of Composition." *Perspectives on Research and Scholarship in Composition.* Ed. Ben W. McClelland and Timothy R. Donovan. New York: MLA, 1985. 6–25.

Brodkey, Linda. "Modernism and the Scene(s) of Writing." *College English* 49 (1987): 396–418.

Brooke, Robert. "Control in Writing: Flower, Derrida, and Images of the Writer." *College English* 51 (1989): 405–17.

Bruffee, Kenneth. "Collaborative Learning and the 'Conversation of Mankind.'" *College English* 46 (1984): 77–81.

————. "Social Construction, Language, and the Authority of Knowledge: A Bibliographical Essay." *College English* 48 (1986): 773–90.

Burke, Kenneth. *Language as Symbolic Action: Essays on Life, Literature, and Method.* Berkeley: U of California P, 1966.

Clark, Suzanne. Personal communication.

Clark, Suzanne, and Lisa Ede. "Collaboration, Resistance, and the Teaching of Writing." *The Right to Literacy.* Ed. Andrea A. Lunsford, Helene Moglen, and James Slevin. New York: MLA, 1990. 276–85.

Coles, William E., Jr. *The Plural I: The Teaching of Writing.* New York: Holt, 1978.

Cooper, Marilyn M. "The Ecology of Writing." *College English* 48 (1986): 364–75.

D'Angelo, Frank. *A Conceptual Theory of Rhetoric.* Cambridge, MA: Winthrop, 1975.

Elbow, Peter. *Writing with Power: Techniques for Mastering the Writing Process.* New York: Oxford UP, 1981.

————. *Writing Without Teachers.* New York: Oxford UP, 1973.

Faigley, Lester A. "Competing Theories of Process: A Critique and a Proposal." *College English* 48 (1986): 527–42.

Flower, Linda. *Problem-Solving Strategies for Writing.* 2nd ed. San Diego: Harcourt, 1985.

Flower, Linda, and John R. Hayes. "The Cognition of Discovery: Defining a Rhetorical Problem." *College Composition and Communication* 31 (1980): 21–32.

Fulkerson, Richard. "Four Philosophies of Composition." *College Composition and Communication* 31 (1979): 343–48.

Gere, Anne Ruggles. *Writing Groups: History, Theory, and Implications.* Carbondale: Southern Illinois UP, 1987.

Graff, Gerald. *Professing Literature: An Institutional History.* Chicago: U of Chicago P, 1987.

Graff, Gerald, and William E. Cain. "Peace Plan for the Canon Wars." *The Nation* 6 (March 1989): 310, 313.

Harris, Joseph, "The Idea of Community in the Study of Writing." *College Composition and Communication* 40 (1989): 11–22.

Heath, Shirley Brice. *Ways with Words: Language, Life, and Work in Communities and Classrooms.* Cambridge, England: Cambridge UP, 1983.

Hillocks, George, Jr. *Research on Written Composition: New Directions for Teaching.* Urbana, IL: National Conference on Research in English and ERIC, 1986.

Howry, Bill. "Teacher Perceptions of Teaching Writing as a Process." Unpublished paper.

Jarratt, Susan C., and Nedra Grogan. "The Splitting Image: Postmodern Feminism and the Ethics of *ethos*." Unpublished essay.

Kameen, Paul. "Reworking the Rhetoric of Composition." *Pre/Text* 1 (1980): 73–92.

Lauer, Janice. "Heuristics and Composition." *Contemporary Rhetoric: A Conceptual Background with Readings*. Ed. W. Ross Winterowd. New York: Harcourt, 1975. 79–87.

LeFevre, Karen. *Invention as a Social Act*. Carbondale: Southern Illinois UP: 1987.

Macrorie, Ken. *Uptaught*. Rochelle Park, NJ: Hayden, 1970.

Murray, Donald M. *Write to Learn*. 3rd ed. Fort Worth: Holt, 1990.

Phelps, Louise Wetherbee. *Composition as a Human Science: Contributions to the Self-Understanding of a Discipline*. New York: Oxford UP, 1988.

Reither, James A. "Writing and Knowing: Toward Redefining the Writing Process." *College English* 47 (1985): 620–28.

Reither, James A., and Douglas Vipond. "Writing as Collaboration." *College English* 51 (1989): 855–67.

Scribner, Sylvia, and Michael Cole. "Unpackaging Literacy." *Perspectives on Literacy*. Ed. Eugene R. Kintgen, Barry M. Kroll, and Mike Rose. Carbondale: Southern Illinois UP, 1988. 57–70.

"Statement of Principles and Standards for the Postsecondary Teaching of Writing." *College Composition and Communication* 40 (1989): 329–36.

Stewart, Donald C. "Textbooks Revisited." *Research in Composition and Rhetoric: A Bibliographic Sourcebook*. Ed. Michael G. Moran and Ronald F. Lunsford. Westport, CT: Greenwood, 1984. 453–68.

Street, Brian V. *Literacy in Theory and Practice*. Cambridge, England: Cambridge UP, 1984.

Warnock, John. "The Writing Process." *Research on Composition and Rhetoric: A Bibliographic Sourcebook*. Ed. Michael C. Moran and Ronald F. Lunsford. Westport, CT: Greenwood, 1984. 3–26.

Young, Richard E. "Concepts of Art and the Teaching of Writing." *The Rhetorical Tradition and Modern Writing*. Ed. James J. Murphy. New York: MLA, 1982. 130–41.

The Politics of the Profession

James F. Slevin

GEORGETOWN UNIVERSITY

Angela Dowell, just completing her Ph.D. in English, specializing in rhetoric and composition, is about to enter the profession. Of course, in many ways she has already been "in" the profession—as a graduate student, and even as an undergraduate major. But by our usual ways of talking about these matters, we would consider her just now on the verge: she is considering a teaching position at a college. It is in the context of this imagined situation that I ask all readers—graduate students, new faculty, old faculty, administrators—to explore the professional politics of teaching writing. I am constructing these very specific circumstances to open up a discussion, not to conclude one. Angela Dowell's situation simply provides the occasion for introducing and exploring a range of issues facing teachers and scholars in the field.

The politics of writing instruction is not just *about* writing and its teaching; it *happens,* more often than not, *in* writing. We live and work among such documents as the four I will focus on in the next few pages, but these are only a very small sampling of the letters and memos and reports, the articles and reviews and readers' comments, the curricula and catalog copy and proposals, that fill our lives.[1] These kinds of documents are part of an ongoing conversation that has power as its constant subtext. This is so even when the conversation is thoroughly candid and respectful, the conversants generous and good-willed—in short, even when we are being, in the current phrase, good citizens. We are in this conversation, like it or not, from the day we begin graduate study, and our decisions are always a part of this realm of discourse— embedded in it, shaped by it. What we can imagine for ourselves is in profound ways dependent on what this conversation imagines for us, and any departure from its norms depends first of all on a critical perception of the institutional norms, assumptions, and power relations that operate within it.

The four documents I am presenting are all parts of Angela Dowell's job search. Although fictional, each has its original in a real document I have seen, and all of them are quite conventional.

A. MLA *Job Information List,* October, 1991

English Department   September 22, 1991
Eastern State University

The department has four openings, all tenure-track positions at the assistant professor level.

(1) Eighteenth-Century Literature.
(2) American Literature, with preferred specialization in African-American literature.
(3) Literary Theory, with preferred specialization in feminist theory.
(4) Rhetoric and Composition, to include responsibility for directing Freshman Writing Program.

Send application letter and CV to Professor Eric Knightly, English Department Chairman, by November 15. ESU is an AA/EOE employer and encourages applications from all minority groups.

B.

Office of the Provost
Eastern State University
February 9, 1992

Ms. Angela Dowell
2333 Samson Street
Arcadia, CA 99488

Dear Ms. Dowell:

It is with great pleasure that I write to offer you the position discussed during your campus visit last month. The English Department met and voted to recommend this offer, and university administrators concur with equal enthusiasm.

Professor Knightly, the English Department chairman, will write to confirm the details of your appointment. I wish simply to specify that it will be an assistant professor position on the tenure track, that it includes your appointment as director of Freshman Writing, that you will receive a three-year contract subject to renewal upon a third-year review, and that you will be eligible for tenure after six years of full-time teaching.

We are delighted to extend this offer, and I look forward to receiving your favorable response as soon as possible. Eastern State certainly needs you.

Sincerely,

Arthur Magnix
Provost

cc: Eric Knightly, English Department

C.

English Department
Eastern State University
February 14, 1992

Ms. Angela Dowell
2333 Samson Street
Arcadia, CA 99488

Dear Angela:

Let me say right off that I am delighted we can make you this offer, and the department eagerly awaits your acceptance. Art Magnix has requested that I write to you clarifying, from the department's perspective, the terms of your appointment.

As we both agree, the Writing Program needs not only a Director but direction, which is what we hope from you. Please be assured that you have the department's complete support, for we consider the program one of our major responsibilities. As Director, you will have the opportunity to appoint and review a staff of very talented, dedicated graduate students and adjunct instructors, to implement and revise the Freshman Writing Curriculum, and to monitor the system of placement and exit examinations. Because of these administrative duties, your teaching load will be reduced by one course per semester.

Your initial appointment as Director of Freshman Writing and as a member of the department, for three years, is subject to review by the tenured members of the department. There is no reason to be concerned about this stipulation. These reviews are customary, designed to assist you in your preparation for your tenure application, and worked out in consultation with you. We have every confidence that you will succeed admirably in the three areas of scholarship, teaching, and service that structure these reviews.

I am enclosing the description of the Writing Program from the department's governance document. We are very much looking forward to your contributions to the effectiveness of this program. If you have any questions or concerns, please give me a call.

Yours truly,

Eric Knightly
English Department Chairman

cc: Arthur Magnix, Provost

D.   Eastern State University Freshman Writing Program

The Freshman Writing Program offers basic introductory courses to all ESU freshmen who do not pass a placement examination offered at the beginning of the fall semester. *English 101* provides students with an opportunity to develop their skills in the discovery of their ideas and in the preparation of papers that organize and clearly communicate those ideas. *English 102* provides students with an opportunity to develop their abilities as readers of both literary and non-literary works and as writers of analytical essays. These courses are the only two courses required of all ESU freshmen, who must either place out of them or pass them (and the program-wide exit exam) with a grade of C or better. Both courses rely on a workshop approach, with attention to the writing process and the conventions of college-level writing. Their purpose is to prepare students for writing across the curriculum throughout their four years at ESU.

The FWP is monitored by a committee of English Department faculty, chaired by the Director of Freshman Writing, who is a member of the department and a specialist in rhetoric and composition. This committee will be made up of the Director, four faculty members, one adjunct instructor, and one graduate student representative. It is charged with reviewing the FWP and reporting to the Department Curriculum Committee any recommendations for change.

These documents make clear that Angela Dowell will be entering not simply a vocation but a profession. Eastern State University is both a forum for the intellectual pleasures of teaching and research and a site where different visions of knowledge, learning, and the aims of education will come into conflict. As an untenured faculty member, she will be deeply vulnerable to this conflict; that's a fact.

If we could imagine Dowell as Candide, then the story of her entanglements in these various documents would be simpler, allowing us the pleasures of utopian speculation or dystopic satire. Such perspectives of innocence enrich our literary *apercus,* evoking for us a set of ideals from which we might measure current realities. But these genres too often substitute longing or rage for understanding and deciding. So I choose instead a commentary that will try to think about—unpack— these various bits of writing that find our protagonist positioned to decide whether or not to accept the "opportunity" that Provost Magnix and Chairman Knightly offer her. My point is not to make that choice for her, but to suggest some of the issues and provide some of the information that might help her make such a decision or help anyone advise a colleague faced with such a choice.[2]

The Changing Culture of English Departments

These documents are perfectly commonplace. Precisely because they are so ordinary, they reflect most clearly a series of contradictions and conflicts that mark the life of the profession right now, and it will be the burden of the following sections to consider these contradictions.

Let's begin at the beginning, with the announcement of the job. This is how the profession communicates a future to its young. In a field that among other things studies eloquence in all its forms, we announce ourselves in the spare, often grotesque genre of the paid advertisement in the Modern Language Association's *Job Information List,* published quarterly. It seems a meat-market approach, a commodification of intellectual labor so gross that we hesitate to elevate it with analysis. But it is worth noting that this "market quarterly" originated in a radical critique, in the late 1960s, of hiring practices that relied all too often on the "old boy" network, with positions often "advertised" through contacts with only the most prestigious professors at only the most prestigious graduate schools. The *JIL* was designed to democratize, if not the awarding of faculty positions, at least the opportunity to seek those positions. And, ironic as it may seem, the *JIL* reflects a democratizing of the profession that is apparent as well in the four positions listed in this particular ad.

The range of positions here points to changes in the discipline that mark both its increasing emphasis on specialization and its broadening of the fields of inquiry that get "certified" by its Ph.D. programs. This change testifies to the initiatives of both established and younger scholars who are taking us in new directions in both the content of what we study and the methods upon which our study depends. Different writers are being read in different ways, now.

Any announcement like this one most likely comes out of a series of complicated negotiations within the department and the university.[3] Two of the positions would seem to represent compromises—with more established categories (theory and American literature) qualified by "preferred specializations" that identify somewhat less mainstream critical approaches, though neither would qualify any longer as "marginal." Taken together, the four positions reveal a kind of fragmentation in how departments go about defining themselves—employing categories based on historical period, national literature (and subcategories therein), and different kinds of historical knowledge and theoretical orientation. It would be naive to think that departments do not have some hierarchy in mind when they construct such different *kinds* of positions. And, as it happens, this hierarchy is reproduced in the very sequence of this particular listing. Despite all the changes that have occurred, the historical periodization of national literatures still dominates our ways of imagining the needs of our departments.

For someone like Angela Dowell, interested in the teaching and study of writing, the listing must seem inevitable, yet strange. "Rhetoric and composition" is quite clearly marked here as a field, listed along with these others as areas in which one can—and so is expected to—specialize. Apparently, rhetoric and composition possesses an intellectual substance and a body of knowledge, conforming in this way to a sense of the field she has gained from graduate study, conferences, and academic journals. But the listing specifies as well—as virtually no other field-listing ever does—administrative responsibilities, and these are understood as somehow "included" in the nature of the field and so the job: "to include . . . directing Freshman Writing." That is, the job that interests her is portrayed here as a discipline that involves institutional "responsibility" and service in ways that are not (or at least not so clearly) noted in the other listings.

We will look in a moment at some of the more unfortunate consequences of this way of understanding the field, with particular attention to the sometimes unreasonable expectations it engenders. But for the moment I want to suggest that this position may not really be an anomaly in the particular configuration of listings set forth in this ad. That is, the larger cultural and social concerns of rhetoric and composition place it among a number of areas of the profession concerned with the ways in which intellectual work can critique and reshape the immediate institutional circumstances in which this work occurs. The effort to redefine academic institutions marks the work of many areas of English Studies in our time—not just rhetoric and composition, but feminist studies, African-American studies, colonial and post-colonial discourse studies, and increasingly even American studies. What they have in common— and what might serve as a basis for a new order of our profession—is both a concern with history and social contexts and also a kind of activism, a merging of scholarship and praxis. They share a sense that the work of research and publication is inseparable from the work of shaping institutional structures such as the department, the university, and programs that connect the academy with the "outside" world. That these fields might have solid reason to affiliate—in scholarly projects and in political action within and on behalf of the university—is something that seems to me a quite conspicuous possibility inherent in this announcement. There is no saying for sure of course; but these jobs, though conceived through the old mechanisms of specialization and periodization, suggest a department well worth the attention of Angela Dowell, who obviously decided in any event that Eastern State was worth a letter of application.

Writing Programs and University Governance

The letters announcing the success of Dowell's application reflect two features of university governance. First, responsibilities are dispersed across various levels of the university. Second, power finally resides with the highest level of administration, with other levels serving in an advisory capacity. As you can see, the provost makes this appointment: departments, department chairs, and even deans just advise in this and many other matters.[4] While departments generally get their wishes in hiring, the peculiar circumstances of Dowell's appointment make the matter somewhat more complicated.

Dowell is likely to be flattered by the last line of the Provost's letter:

"Eastern State certainly needs you." She is not just being appointed, she is being wooed, and not just by the department chair but by the higher administration as well. Both see her as serving their interests, the former as director of Freshman English, the latter as director of the only university-wide requirement, designed to "prepare students for writing . . . throughout their four years at ESU." This situation makes the role of the writing specialist, especially someone charged with particular administrative responsibilities, all the more difficult to describe and assess. For, if Angela Dowell decides to accept this position, she may very well find her allegiances split significantly.

Let us step back a moment to explore a range of ways that writing instruction and writing programs can be situated within an institution, and let us begin with a neglected but actually the most common situation of composition teaching. Since most college faculty members receive their training at large Ph.D. institutions, they are usually surprised to learn that the average English department in this country has about nine faculty members. It is fair to say that the "usual" English department is located at a small college, with a small faculty, all of whom are assigned the same teaching loads and similar responsibilities for all levels of the curriculum. So here, the famed literature/composition battleground is felt, if at all, only in the inner recesses of each teacher's feelings about his or her work. By and large, freshman courses—usually, though not always, composition courses—are taught by all faculty members, from the oldest teacher to the newest hot-shot Ph.D. In the glaring spotlights of Ph.D. programs, we may easily forget that these liberal arts colleges still exist, offering careers in teaching that often mesh with some teachers' earliest visions of what a life in the academy could mean to them.

At larger institutions, the place of composition teaching is more complicated, and these complications are at the heart of the century-long struggle for governance that marks higher education. Let me suggest several typical arrangements. In the first, of which Eastern State University is an example, the Writing Program is housed in the English department; as Writing Program Director, Angela Dowell would report directly to the department chair, who controls the entire department budget (including her program's) and assigns teaching and administrative responsibilities. The department chair in turn reports to the dean, who in turn is responsible to Art Magnix, Provost.

Such an arrangement has distinct advantages. For one, Dowell will have a home in an academic department, and this can be helpful in matters of tenure and promotion. Her work for the Writing Program might be seen as significant department service, as enhancing the contributions of the department to the university's well-being. Her third-year review and tenure application will be handled routinely, with the department's recommendation proceeding through a series of levels (the undergraduate and in some cases graduate dean and a university-wide tenure and promotion committee) before a final decision is made, either by the provost or the president.

On the other hand, governance, especially because she is untenured, may be problematic, even if Eastern State already boasts a supportive group of tenured composition specialists or fellow-travelers. Her budget requests will compete for the chair's attention with other department needs. It is unlikely that a program defined in terms of a university-wide requirement that serves all freshmen and only freshmen will have as much "clout" with him as more pressing demands (for research support, smaller class sizes at the elective level, stronger support for the M.A. program, and so on). And given that the first six years of Dowell's life will be spent "under review," she is not going to be in a very strong position to press for needed funding and changes, since any pressure will place her in conflict with senior colleagues having their own agendas.

Envisioning this predicament, Dowell may be tempted by other academic appointments that would establish her within a Writing Program separate from any academic department. It would have its own budget line; as its director Dowell would probably be a faculty member in the English department, but she would report directly to the dean or some other administrator. She would find certain real advantages to this arrangement, foremost among them being that high-level administrators are sometimes more likely to value the work of the Writing Program, esteeming more than would the English department's faculty (or any single department's faculty) the program's important contributions to general education. Moreover, the program could devote itself with uncompromised energy to writing *across* the curriculum.

But there are difficulties here as well. First, under this alternative system, tenure and promotion can often be quite problematic. Even though Dowell would be a member of the English department, her responsibilities would be viewed as "split," and so suffer all the dangers of any split appointment, especially severe in this case since the other side of the "split" is perceived as "mere service." Moreover, competition for funding here is not necessarily less factious and could be more intense. Budgets in such an arrangement depend on the dean, so the Writing Program competes with other programs and with academic departments for support. Like other battles, this too is usually unequal, and while the Writing Program is free of intradepartmental squabbles, its status in the institution is weaker than that of most of its competitors, academic *departments*.

Still another possible arrangement might present itself to Dowell, but it is one that she would surely have to think long and hard about accepting. This position duplicates the previous institutional arrangement, but her status as director would be non-tenure-track—what is commonly called an academic staff position. In cases where her position would not be on a tenure line, job security is often (ironically) less risky, because no decision on tenure would be absolutely required. A series of multi-year contracts would be arranged. But there's a price to pay. Lacking faculty status, she could aspire at best to influence, not power, and she would remain, technically, powerless within the governance system of the institution, unable, for example, to serve in the faculty senate or even to vote in faculty senate elections and meetings. And the absence of any protection of her academic freedom would make her position all the more precarious in times of conflict. These costs also come in matters of program governance, since non-tenure-line directors regularly have limited power in deciding the hiring and retention of teachers or changing the curriculum.

In any event, what is important to notice is that Angela Dowell is being summoned—with an enthusiasm that she takes to be genuine—to a position filled with possible difficulties. In this and other matters we will be taking up, it might be time now for her to negotiate seriously the nature of the position and the ways in which she can secure some authority and security for herself and her program, even during the probationary period leading to her tenure decision. And the nature of the tenure decision itself could surely stand some serious negotiation before she accepts ESU's offer. It is time to ask, for example, precisely what Knightly means when he claims that she will have "the department's complete support." Do they understand what they are asking of her and what it will take genuinely to support that?

Departmental Politics

In going to ESU, Dowell would be entering a department with her three new assistant professor colleagues, with a specialization like theirs, with the same desire to publish and participate at professional conferences as they have, with the same interest in teaching her specialty. Like any graduate student in these highly professional times, she has been trained to do research and has even begun to prepare essays for publication and give a few conference papers. She has ideas about which she wants to write, ideas she wants to explore in courses for majors and graduate students. In the most serious ways, she wants to be sure that she will receive the same research support as her peers, that the journals in which she publishes will receive the respect that theirs do, and that her teaching duties will include, as theirs do, graduate and undergraduate electives that allow her to do what she has been trained to do.

At the same time, she will have additional responsibilities that they do not have and she has been trained in a discipline that, while having a history of two millennia, is nevertheless, in its modern incarnation, perceived as less clearly defined and less established than theirs. These differences are not now—at Eastern State or most other institutions— fully grasped and respected. Some of the features of this misunderstanding deserve consideration, especially as they might bear on Dowell's future at the school.

As her letters from the provost and the department chair indicate, decisions about faculty retention are governed by three categories: teaching, scholarship, and service. The relative weight given to each category varies from institution to institution, but it is fair to say that service is universally the least significant factor, even though a faculty member might choose (or be "asked") to devote most of his or her time to it. It goes without saying that the one-course reduction her chair has awarded will be small relief indeed for a job that could very well consume all of her time. And, when it comes right down to it, no matter how brilliantly she does her job, it is unlikely to count for much toward securing her future. Equally troubling, her uncertain "tenure" at the institution and the general perception that her service will not count are likely to undermine the quality of her work, making this institutional policy self-defeating for both Dowell and Eastern State.

What will count are scholarship and teaching, and their relative importance decidedly varies. All institutions say, with a certain energy that occasionally aspires to eloquence, that teaching "truly matters"; virtually all say that it matters as much as scholarship; and many say that it matters more. That they can say this and often not mean it is a matter of some ethical interest, but it is not a concern that Dowell can dwell on at this moment. Her concern is rather with the measures that are used in making determinations about the quality of teaching and scholarship and how these measures affect specialists in rhetoric and composition.

To measure teaching, colleges and universities have developed elaborate systems of classroom visitations and computerized student evaluation forms. Unfortunately, these measures cannot reliably register what goes on in a writing class, and occasionally the most effective teaching practices are missed or misunderstood. Faculty visitors tend to expect a class in which the teacher maintains a strong intellectual presence (through lecture or controlled discussion) and so shapes the students' learning in immediately visible ways. Student evaluation forms do much the same, geared often toward the lecture as the standard way of "conducting" a class, and setting up implicit norms that overvalue the *teacher's* performance in the classroom and undervalue the students' performance. In significant ways, these norms work against some of the best work that goes on in a writing course. Decentered classrooms, workshop approaches, and lots of individual attention through conferences are simply not "seen" through the current mechanisms of evaluation. The review of Dowell's teaching needs to take into account the special circumstances of the writing classroom.

Securing an adequate evaluation of service will also involve a certain amount of change at most institutions. The Modern Language Association's "Report of the Commission on Writing and Literature" (1988) offers several helpful recommendations, including the possibility that, during renewal and tenure reviews, an outside evaluator be commissioned to visit the campus and evaluate the service contributions of the writing teacher/administrator. This visit would involve observing classes and training workshops, conversing with students and faculty, and examining relevant documents. The Commission recommends that, just as the "weighting" of service with respect to other factors should be adjusted for rhetoric and composition faculty, so too this outside evaluation should be afforded the same status as evaluations of research during the review.

The evaluation of research, of course, is itself something of a problem for many in rhetoric and composition. The MLA Commission Report describes some of these problems and offers four recommendations that modify the definition of research and expand the range of intellectual and professional work that gets included in this category. Though such recommendations come from the MLA, they are still often neglected or resisted by its members, who constitute the dominant figures in the profession generally and in most English departments. In summary fashion, the Report recommends that colleges and universities should: (1) recognize that composition textbooks are often the most valuable ways of communicating the results of serious scholarship, and so accord them the same status as other scholarly genres; (2) resist certain competitive and individualistic assumptions about research in the humanities, and so reward the kind of collaborative work that increasingly marks the field of rhetoric and composition; (3) count as serious professional contributions knowledge disseminated through workshops and seminars for teachers at all levels, including pre-college educators; (4) recognize that certain kinds of administrative work can be a form of scholarship, dependent on research and capable of reshaping our understanding of the discipline.

It is a healthy sign that the profession has begun to counter the unrealistic expectations that the academy has for its writing specialists, and to initiate official forms of support for their work. That some of our major journals (*College English, College Composition and Communication, Rhetoric Review,* and others) have initiated policies of blind submission and anonymous review makes cases for tenure and promotion stronger. It is helpful, too, that more scholars in this field have attained full professorships at prestigious universities, since their outside evaluation of a tenure candidate's research now carries more weight. In general, the chances for tenure of rhetoric and composition faculty are improving. Not so fortunate, however, are those off the "tenure track," who make up the majority of college writing teachers in this country. Angela Dowell, who may not have met them yet, will soon become closely acquainted with them if she accepts this particular offer.

Politics of Exploitation:
The Writing Program's Professional Underclass

Eric Knightly's letter clarifying her appointment quite clearly states a set of hiring practices that Angela Dowell will inherit as Director of Freshman Writing. ESU's writing faculty—a misnomer, since they are precisely *non*-faculty—comprises almost exclusively graduate students and adjunct instructors. In taking on this position, Dowell will find herself responsible not just *to* the various levels of administration that will eventually review her work but *for* a teaching staff of sometimes experienced, sometimes utterly inexperienced instructors who have in common only their exploitation.

This exploitation has been addressed by the Conference on College Composition and Communication in its "Statement of Principles and Standards for the Postsecondary Teaching of Writing," issued in October 1989. Since then endorsed by many other professional associations, including the Executive Council of the MLA, this document establishes a foundation for challenging a series of practices that are now endemic to higher education.

We know, for example, that 50% of the teachers at two-year colleges are part-time, that 25% of the faculty at four-year colleges are part-time, and that a significant portion of the rest have only a temporary, non-tenure-track appointment. And we know that even at those "distinguished" departments offering the Ph.D., over 50% of the teaching staff is made up of part-timers, TAs, and temporary appointments. Almost always, it is composition that gets taught by those teachers in the least privileged positions. The circumstances of their work are dreadful: they have little autonomy and no secured academic freedom; they have virtually no access to travel funds or support for their research; they lack even the most basic needs of writing teachers (sufficient office space, clerical assistance, and supplies, for example). And like many composition teachers, tenure-line or not, they often are confronted with classes that are too large and with teaching loads that are too demanding.

Graduate teaching assistants have similar difficulties. The size of many graduate programs is often dictated by the number of TAs needed to staff the Freshman Writing Program. Graduate students are "calculated" as a source of inexpensive labor, and they are used (or rather misused) accordingly. They often must teach courses for which they are not yet prepared, and they frequently must teach more courses than they can reasonably handle if they are to make satisfactory progress toward their degrees.

What these practices reveal is a debasement of what it means to teach writing. While both the provost and the English Department chair at ESU speak with enthusiasm of the importance of the Writing Program and the need for new directions, they still support (and in many ways depend on) this program's remaining marginal to the "higher" matters of higher education. In some ways, at this time, they cannot afford to think otherwise. The debasement of "writing" rationalizes the debased status of the faculty who teach it and the base salaries they receive.

The CCCC "Statement of Principles and Standards" addresses these abuses and calls for significant reform. It begins with the status of the teaching of writing, and with the respect accorded both teaching and research in rhetoric and composition, because the connection between scholarship and teaching is of critical importance within the culture of the academy at this time. In demanding respect for the scholarly work done in this field, it connects the importance of that work to needed reforms in the academy's employment practices. So it asserts that writing courses should be staffed by tenure-line faculty; that graduate students should be treated as *students* and supported for their study, not their teaching; that the percentage of part-time faculty should be no more than 10% of the teaching staff at any given time; and that the treatment of any part-time faculty should include pro-rated salaries, adequate preparation and support, a role in governance and evaluation, and in some cases security of employment.

While these guidelines may seem, in the present landscape of exploitation, slightly quixotic, they represent a set of norms to which higher education should be made to adhere, even if the effort to do so takes more time than we would hope. How much time Angela Dowell will have, and the pressure on her to pay attention to many other matters (including the demands of publication), are genuinely open questions, questions she will have to weigh and answer for herself. What is certain is this: she must at least ponder these matters and make difficult political choices about where she stands and how and in what areas she will move toward change. For change will be required, if only because increasing opportunities for tenure-line positions will make it increasingly difficult to retain the same quality of teacher for part-time positions and the same quality of graduate student for an M.A. program like ESU's.

In her efforts to improve the status of writing teachers and teaching on her campus, Dowell can find valuable information and often support from other organizations concerned about reform. The MLA's Association of Departments of English, for example, has fairly up-to-date information about employment practices at English departments across the country. The American Association of University Professors publishes policy statements concerning faculty rights as they relate to issues of academic freedom and tenure, and most campuses have an AAUP chapter, whose president might be a resource in working for change. Increasingly, regional accrediting agencies are aware that the part-time situation has gotten out of hand, especially in English, math, and foreign language departments. Dowell can use all these resources to advantage when her university is preparing for accreditation visits. All these organizations can easily be contacted, and all have proven cooperative in the past.[5]

Not everything will be possible at once, and different institutions are vulnerable to reform in different areas. Dowell may find, for example, that it will be easier to increase writing teachers' autonomy and upgrade their participation in governance; or she may find that raising salaries finds less resistance among a faculty very protective of its authority. These changes, however minimal at first, will make a difference in the long run. They will be powerfully assisted by any changes she can make in the Writing Program curriculum. Those teaching in it will be taken more seriously and rewarded more justly to the extent that it becomes more fully respected. So now, curricular politics.

Curricular Politics: Moving Toward Change

Throughout this volume, we find several representations of rhetoric and composition as a field, variant configurations of its sub-fields, and explanations of the differences among these sub-fields in terms of their competing interests, emphases, methodologies, and even ideologies. Angela Dowell, based on some combination of personal conviction and training, will locate her intellectual work within this array of possibilities. The degree of tact with which she will choose to counter or encounter different points of view seems very much a matter of temperament, and in matters of scholarship she will find a broad tolerance for even the harshest rhetoric of dispute and idea-assassination. In her publications and conference papers, she can address her professional colleagues pretty much as she likes.

How she manages her relationships at home, at Eastern State, is another matter entirely. Here, different ideas have immediate and palpable consequences, not just for the students, whose education is shaped by those ideas in the form of the curriculum, but for the faculty, whose intellectual and professional and even personal identities are invested in that curriculum. In effect, faculty members want to be its authors; they want it to reflect their convictions. These matters and how they get talked about count heavily. Solutions for curricular problems can emerge only through Dowell's continuing dialogue and negotiation with her colleagues. What she might anticipate in entering that dialogue, however, can be suggested with some degree of confidence.

That Dowell will be entering an arena of some disagreement, or at least contradictions, is apparent even from the few documents at her disposal. English 101 and English 102, courses hardly unique to Eastern State, represent a murky yoking of different, perhaps ultimately incompatible, ways of understanding the teaching of writing. Although the two courses are attentive to the students' writing process and the pedagogical value of seeing the classroom as a workshop, they seem, finally, "service" courses: "Their purpose is to *prepare* students. . . ." No matter what might actually go on in them, the institution regards them as "preps." Although the courses are concerned with discovering ideas and communicating them, both activities are described as "skills," so the nature of the work that students do in these courses is seen as inferior to the work of other courses. Although asserting their relevance and importance to a university education, the program description embeds a sense that these are not subjects necessary to everyone's university education but only to those who cannot pass a placement exam: that is, no matter how bright the students, a kind of remediation is implied here, bringing students up to speed. Implicit in these versions of 101 and 102 is the assumption that this is not work that really ought to go on at this level.

The use of placement and especially exit examinations points to an even deeper, and more troubling, institutional purpose for these courses. The historical analyses of Richard Ohmann and James Berlin, among others, have made clear that these kinds of courses have served, for at least a century, an aim not wholly consonant with those professed by specialists in rhetoric and composition today. For these critics, to different degrees, these courses have functioned to socialize students into the linguistic conventions and social habits of the dominant class. Because the university guarantees that it will provide society with well-behaved and efficient contributors to the operations of corporate capitalism, "Freshman Comp" must serve one of two functions: either it begins the process of socializing students, or it serves as a gatekeeper, weeding out those deemed inappropriately prepared to enter the various "communities" that make up the university.

In some ways, then, the courses with their exit examination serve as a check both on students and on their teachers. Both are under scrutiny here in this centrally monitored process of surveillance. For the courses' teachers, the exit exam just reinforces their generally debased professional status. They lack even the authority to evaluate their students. For the students, the courses and exam constitute the perfect site for surveillance and socialization; here the students' participation in the life of the academy (here they *have* to "put things in writing") can be most powerfully monitored and controlled. ESU's emphasis on evaluation reflects these larger institutional missions. What it rewards, under these circumstances, is the ability not necessarily to write but to pass, to construct a self in writing that will move one through the gate that bars the unworthy.

Understanding in this light the curriculum she will inherit, Angela Dowell will need to deal with a wide variety of views that will complicate or obstruct any changes she will want to make. I won't try to envision all the possibilities here, but offer just a sampling. Pressing from above and from without will be those who are perfectly satisfied with the course and its purposes as they are now defined; they will object only to the execution of this "mission" ("Why can't my students write clearly and correctly?"). Here, Dowell is likely to get caught in a web of disputes about the purposes of the course and the course's relationship to the kinds and quality of students being admitted to Eastern State. She will also encounter at least some who continue to think that the function of Freshman English is the teaching of literature and who may very well seek a return to this, especially if Dowell persuades tenured colleagues to teach in the freshman program. As it is, English 102 could very easily be, in the hands of certain faculty members, a course in the close reading of literary texts.

Many of Dowell's colleagues, especially in the kind of English department reflected in the job announcement, will want to resist both of these conservative tendencies, and they can serve as valuable allies in Dowell's effort to give a new direction (that, after all, is what her appointment letters ask her to do) to the Freshman Writing Program. Some of her literature colleagues may derive from their own research and experiences in the classroom ways of understanding the importance of "writing" that will bear on the very conception of her program. Feminist scholars, especially in literature, linguistics, and psychology, have argued that certain linear forms of organization enforce a way of thinking and writing that is inimical to women students, and these colleagues may have a role to play in reconceiving the freshman curriculum. Researchers who are studying the way universities generally dis-serve their (increasing) non-mainstream student populations (minority students, foreign students, students from lower social classes) will also have much to contribute.

Such allies can be helpful, but Dowell would expect to find most helpful of all, of course, her colleagues in rhetoric and composition. Unfortunately, they are more likely to agree on what's wrong with the current system than on what might be substituted for it. All might agree, for example, that the point of a writing course is student empowerment, the opening of each classroom (and in that way the university) to all students. They might even agree that the courses should be devoted to rethinking what goes on at the university.

But their ways of arriving at this empowerment, indeed what they take empowerment to mean, are likely to differ, as will the different curricula and pedagogies that derive from their convictions. Some will no doubt argue for a freshman curriculum that focuses on expressive writing and the development of students' individual voices. Others will argue that freshman English should afford students a critical perception of the constraints and genuine intellectual possibilities of academic discourse, providing them with the opportunity to use for their own purposes, and not just simulate for the purposes of the institution, the genres of the academy. Others will argue for a radical liberatory pedagogy that politicizes the aims of the courses. There might even be a small knot of anarchists who will argue that the problem with Freshman English is that it exists at all, that it ought to be done away with, leaving the socializing of students and the weeding out of the inadequate to some other, less ethical, department, if one can be found.

Dowell may find, in fact, that nearly all these conflicting positions are represented on the Freshman Writing Program Committee that she chairs. And given the Gothic administrative twist that has this committee virtually powerless in itself, reporting to a Department Curriculum Committee, she may sometimes feel that change is impossible. Negotiating all these areas of disagreement within her department and beyond it, drawing in others from the department and across the campus who may assist her, and doing all of this while still making sure that the current system gets administered with some care, may provide her with all the turmoil she needs to contemplate another career. Things will certainly seem, on occasion, bleak.

It is precisely this bleakness, however, that makes the work so important. Dowell does not need to be committed to "pluralism" to believe, finally, that the university is valuable precisely to the extent that it brings together and empowers a faculty with a genuine diversity of points of view. Moreover, institutional resistance usually occurs for significant reasons, because something fundamental is at stake. The politics of teaching writing is about the most important issues now confronting higher education: it is about the kinds of students who get to attend and to succeed at the college and university, about the authenticity of our commitment to democratic education; it is about what happens to them there and how their writing can make a difference for them; and it is about our understanding of what it means to know and change what is claimed to be known.

The field of rhetoric and composition has emerged in our own time with these aims very much in the forefront of its concerns.[6] It has emerged, that is, as a form of educational and political reform. It has asserted that student and faculty commitments need to be freed from the institutionally established purposes to which they have been reduced. It has addressed broad questions about the aims of education and the shape of various educational institutions—from the social institution we call the "classroom" to the general education curriculum to the discipline itself. The catch phrases with which we are all familiar—writing as process, writing to learn, writing as a way of thinking, writing as a way of knowing, writing as empowerment—are responses to a concern, not that students are incompetent or unprepared, but rather that they are often led *by their educations* to be uncaring—about ideas, about their own learning, and often about other matters that transcend the more immediate interests of any particular classroom. Concern with "access" and "empowerment" is finally a concern with students' alienation from the very institutions that are supposed to make possible their intellectual lives.

Finally, the politics of teaching writing should not be merely a defensive maneuver, protecting our turf, rationalizing our self-interest; it should rather involve initiating change that is deeply needed in American higher education. I am thinking, broadly, of the entire academy, more narrowly of individual colleges and universities, and more narrowly still of English Studies and the English departments where many rhetoric and composition specialists teach. For in considering the politics of teaching writing, we need to be concerned, finally, about imagining and enacting new possibilities for ourselves and the profession. Our aim, then, should be not simply to re-situate ourselves within institutions but, in doing so, to reconceive and reconstruct those institutions.

So perhaps the most fundamental question is this: Has Angela Dowell been prepared for this most important work?

Preparing for the Work of Change

Does she, for example, know what it means to accept this position? If she knows what it means, in some sense, will she know what to do? If she could do what she wanted, would she know what that was—and how to make it happen?

I have suggested that the politics of teaching writing must be a politics of change and reform, not adaptation and accommodation. Graduate training currently makes such a politics most difficult, for in failing to assist students in preparing themselves to initiate change, the profession leaves them virtually helpless in their efforts to survive, among other things, the first six years of their careers, that tenure-probationary period meant to test their mettle. Too many graduate students, including rhetoric and composition specialists, leave graduate school without a clue.

Change can begin at the graduate level, and one important purpose of this volume is to contribute to such change. Our graduate students' education, constrained by the pressures of scholarly "specialization," does too little to prepare young professionals to take charge of the wide range of responsibilities that so many departments will require of them, and this is especially true in our field. Students need the opportunity to set the work of rhetoric and composition in particular, and more generally the work of English Studies and the academy, in larger professional and theoretical contexts. As in part a professional degree program, the Ph.D. curriculum should incorporate formal occasions not just for developing scholars and teachers but for inquiring about the profession of scholarship and teaching and about the institutions in which they occur.[7]

A graduate seminar preparing new faculty members to meet their responsibilities and envision change would want to begin with a broad historical analysis of change in our discipline. It would trace how we have narrowed our concern to reading canonical works, to the detriment of our understanding of how those texts came to be (the process of textual production) and to be deemed worthy of our scrutiny (the process of canonization). It would investigate not just how to teach writing but the history of writing instruction, including its role in socializing new student populations historically called "remedial." It would draw on the work of other disciplines (psychology, linguistics, and much of contemporary literary theory) as they contribute to our changing understanding of textuality. And it might even address the current preoccupation of nearly all humanistic disciplines with "discursive practices" by bringing to bear on this question major texts from the rhetorical tradition. As a forum for disciplined inquiry about the aims of education and the meaning of liberal learning, this course would provide a crucial preparation for graduate students embarking on a new career.

Recent efforts, particularly of Berlin, Graff, Ohmann, Lentricchia, and Fish, to situate scholarship and teaching within their institutional settings and larger historical contexts provide a solid framework for organizing such a seminar. It could thereby consider the origins of English Studies in relation not only to the system of departmental governance but to the norm of specialization and the ideology of professionalism that rationalizes it. It could investigate the ways in which the teaching of writing became incorporated within and subordinated to other intellectual purposes in higher education. In such an inquiry, it could examine historically how specific curricular arrangements were formed and how one's own theoretical inquiry into the writing process, authorship, canonicity, textuality, and genre can be brought to bear in understanding and reconceiving those formations, with particular attention to the composition curriculum. And of more immediate consequence, it would examine how the profession's system of rewards and accompanying constraints (research expectations, teaching loads, evaluation procedures) came into being and how these rewards/constraints mold both the intellectual lives and professional careers of university faculty. These hardly exhaust the possible topics of such seminars; others can easily be imagined. The aim, however, would be to pose those questions that will empower graduate students as agents in reconceiving and shaping the institutions whose faculties they will join.

With such a program, Angela Dowell would be no less prepared for her career, and she would have made herself far more ready for her work. She would know, at least, what she needs to find out. Eric Knightly's letter asked her to call if she had any questions or concerns.

With the right training, she'd know how to take him up on that offer. With the best training, she'd know to call collect.

Notes

1. I am talking now about life in the profession, not in the discipline, and while I take to heart those arguments (by Fish, for example) that virtually equate the two and the writing that proceeds within them both, I am finally persuaded that some crucial distinctions are being neglected.

2. It goes without saying that I can barely begin to unpack all that is going on here. I leave much to my readers.

3. It is *unlikely* that students were consulted in this negotiation, though enrollment patterns may have been studied. Whether or not Eastern State University ought in reality to be hiring specialists in these fields, or specialists at all; whether they should in fact be hiring four people who are gifted teachers with no real desire to publish; whether they should be doing a lot of things that don't necessarily reproduce so-called professional norms is something that may have been mentioned, but was probably not discussed. For a valuable examination of this issue, see Ohmann, *English in America,* chapter 8.

4. It is conceivable that Dowell could be hired—and terminated six years later—by a man she will never meet. It is highly improbable that she and Magnix will ever know one another.

5. Pertinent information—with addresses and phone numbers of such organizations as the AAUP, ADE, and all regional accrediting agencies—appears in *College Composition and Communication* 40 (February 1989): 65–72.

6. For a full development of this position, see my article in *The Politics of Writing Instruction* (Boynton/Cook, Heinemann, 1991).

7. For a more complete discussion of changes needed in our graduate programs, see my article, "Conceptual Frameworks and Curricular Arrangements," *The Future of Doctoral Studies in English* (New York: MLA, 1989), 30–39.

Suggested Readings

Berlin, James. *Rhetoric and Reality: Writing Instruction in American Colleges, 1900–1985.* Carbondale: Southern Illinois UP, 1987.
———. *Writing Instruction in Nineteenth-Century American Colleges.* Carbondale: Southern Illinois UP, 1984.
Bullock, Richard, John Trimbur, and Charles Schuster, eds. *The Politics of*

Writing Instruction. Portsmouth, NH: Boynton/Cook, Heinemann, 1991.

Graff, Gerald. *Professing Literature: An Institutional History*. Chicago: U of Chicago P, 1987.

Lunsford, Andrea, Helene Moglen, and James Slevin, eds. *The Future of Doctoral Studies in English*. New York: MLA, 1989.

Ohmann, Richard. *English in America*. New York: Oxford UP, 1976.

———. *The Politics of Letters*. Middletown, CT: Wesleyan UP, 1987.

Parker, William Riley. "Where Do English Departments Come From?" *College English* 28 (1967): 339–51. Rpt. in *The Writing Teacher's Sourcebook*. Ed. Gary Tate and Edward P. J. Corbett. New York: Oxford UP, 1988.

"Report of the MLA Commission on Writing and Literature." *Profession 88*. New York: MLA, 1988. 70–76.

"Statement of Principles and Standards for Postsecondary Teaching of Writing." *College Composition and Communication* 40 (1989): 329–36.

Works Cited

Berlin, James. *Rhetoric and Reality: Writing Instruction in American Colleges, 1900–1985*. Carbondale: Southern Illinois UP, 1987.

———. *Writing Instruction in Nineteenth-Century American Colleges*. Carbondale: Southern Illinois UP, 1984.

Bullock, Richard, John Trimbur, and Charles Schuster, eds. *The Politics of Writing Instruction*. Portsmouth, NH: Boynton/Cook, Heinemann, 1991.

Fish, Stanley. "Anti-Professionalism." *New Literary History* 17 (1985): 89–108.

———. "Profession Despise Thyself: Fear and Loathing in Literary Studies." *Critical Inquiry* 10 (1983): 349–64.

Graff, Gerald. *Professing Literature: An Institutional History*. Chicago: U of Chicago P, 1987.

Huber, Bettina, and David Laurence. "Report on the 1984–85 Survey of the English Sample." *ADE Bulletin* 93 (Fall 89): 30–43.

Huber, Bettina, and Art Young. "Report on the 1983–84 Survey of English Programs." *ADE Bulletin* 84 (Fall 86): 40–61.

Lentricchia, Frank. *Criticism and Social Change*. Chicago: U of Chicago P, 1983.

Lentricchia, Frank, Sharon Crowley, and Linda Robertson. "Wyoming Resolution." *College English* 49 (1987): 253–58.

Lunsford, Andrea, Helene Moglen, and James Slevin, eds. *The Future of Doctoral Studies in English*. New York: MLA, 1989.

Ohmann, Richard. *English in America.* New York: Oxford UP, 1976.

———. *The Politics of Letters.* Middletown, CT: Wesleyan UP, 1987.

Parker, William Riley. "Where Do English Departments Come From?" *College English* 28 (1967): 339–51. Rpt. in *The Writing Teacher's Sourcebook.* Ed. Gary Tate and Edward P. J. Corbett. New York: Oxford UP, 1988.

"Report of the MLA Commission on Writing and Literature." *Profession 88.* New York: MLA, 1988. 70–76.

Scholes, Robert. *Textual Power: Literary Theory and the Teaching of English.* New Haven: Yale UP, 1985.

"Statement of Principles and Standards for Postsecondary Teaching of Writing." *College Composition and Communication* 40 (1989): 329–36.

A Life in the Profession

Charles Moran

UNIVERSITY OF MASSACHUSETTS AT AMHERST

When the editors of this book asked me to write a chapter titled "A Life in the Profession," I was at first amused—because, at age 54, I feel that I have some life yet left to live. But I was also drawn to the task because I've become just old enough to begin to wonder why it is that my life has taken its particular shape and direction. I am a Ph.D. in English who, trained as a literary scholar, became a writing teacher, a director of a writing program at a research university, a person who attends the annual CCCC meetings with joy and MLA meetings only when he has to. How is it that I have come to the teaching of writing, when all signs told me to avoid this part of the field that is English? My experience tells me that we are as a class excluded, paid less, marginalized by the rest of English. What is it that has led me to join this small band of outcasts? What match between the field and my own history? My own needs?

This essay gives me a chance to address this question for myself and, insofar as it is possible to generalize from the individual to the group, for some others in our discipline. As I look toward the prose I will write, I see the loom of these thoughts on the horizon. We are English, yes, but we are distinguished from our colleagues in literary studies by an empirical bent. We'd rather be close to the place where, as those in the automobile culture would say, the rubber meets the road. We are, moreover, a social crew: not for us monastic years in the library carrel. We need to be working with others, implicated in society. We also want to help people. We want to make things go better, in our classes and beyond. Yet despite our difference, we live, most of us, within English departments, and in some degree of discomfort. Our relationship to English is always interesting, and sometimes difficult.

As I write, I'm assuming that I've been active in making my life what it has been. What one does is a function of identity or "self," but that self is also a function of where one chances to begin—family, its background, its interests—and what happens after the beginning: the inter-section of cultural and economic forces, chance meetings, particular events, influential people. As a person who has chaired an English department, I have come to think that those who achieve Ph.D.s in English are not at all a random set. We are a clear "kind," with shared disposition and character. We likely share, therefore, some aspects of our histories. I'm part of a small group—the group that pursued and completed the Ph.D. in English in the late 1960s. I'm also part of a subset of that group: Ph.D.s in English who have become specialists in the teaching of writing—composition studies, as we now call it. How has this come to pass?

A Beginning

I begin with early signs: in fifth grade, a small boy, young for his grade and small for his age, making it with the means available, helping other students with their math and their "papers," and reading a lot. My early report cards tell me that I missed a lot of school because I was sick. Lots of upper respiratory problems, apparently. Since that time I have run marathons, so I suspect that I was not as sick as the report cards suggest. I do remember reading steadily during these holidays I seem to have made for myself. I dreaded gym because I could not haul myself to the ceiling on the thick rope—a part of the obstacle course that was "gym" for the duration, while our fathers were away fighting World War II. We also tumbled on pre-urethane mats and, with long legs and short torso I was unable to do the required backward somersaults. Later I was called, among other things, "the Little Professor," a reference to Dom DiMaggio, then center fielder for the Red Sox—because of my glasses, not my baseball skills, and because I helped people with their homework. At one point in my early schooling I developed a talent for writing satirical verse, chiefly aimed at the teachers (a safe target) and at the bigger boys in the school (an unsafe target, but satisfying to hit).

I have early memories of writing and reading places: sitting in my grandfather's study, a dark room with ceiling-high bookshelves, a globe in a wooden stand, and a huge-seeming desk with a green pad on it and a paperweight, a cut-and-polished geode that I now have on my desk beside my computer. And I remember reading, in various libraries, in schools and at home, because reading seemed to work better than other

kinds of living. I remember much later meeting a lawyer-friend at his
"club" in Boston and, because he was late, waiting for an hour in the
"writing room" of the club—high ceilings, dark, wooden wainscoting,
shaded lights, small desks, pens, paper, and a French mantel-clock
ticking quietly. I was taken back to libraries of my childhood—not the
activity and metal shelves of the research libraries I've worked in since,
but small home or town or school libraries with comfortable chairs and a
clear sense that one was in another, and safer, world.

In my family, however, reading was something you did after you had
done what was really important—your "work." My mother's father
was a lawyer who put in long hours and was proud of it; my father was a
stockbroker who worked nights and weekends except when he was
levelled by migraine headaches which were, we thought, an extension
of the "hard work" that took place in his office. On weekends we fixed
cars, painted storm windows, did home maintenance. My father had
since 1932 supported his father who, we were told, refused to work
after he had "gone under" in the Great Depression. This grandfather, I
learned to believe, though he was an amateur historian who had published a fair amount, did not support himself and was not, therefore, one
of us.

There was another wing of the family, my father's sister's side, that
included an Aunt Rosalie who taught physics at Bryn Mawr, a Cousin
Nancy who wrote a book on urban education, and Cousin Edwin, who
taught Political Science at the University of New Mexico and has just
published a book on the American intervention in the politics of South
America. So there were, potentially, in-family models for what I was
setting out to be. But these were not, we thought, practical people.
Behind my own family's love of the practical, I now believe, was a need
to be busy and to be with people, not alone. Both of my parents were
prone to depression, as I have found I am myself, and keeping busy has
been a fence, for all of us, against the dark times. My father, my mother
now tells me, would read, chiefly biography, until three or four in the
morning, to postpone the moment when he would finally have to sleep.
My brother is now a microbiologist, with a lab full of intricate machine-
ry and a research team for company. To keep himself busy he is also a
falconer, a musician, and, like our father before him, an amateur automobile racer.

I went off to boarding school in 1948, therefore, with two sets of
aptitudes and inclinations. I was a reader and a writer, and so wrote for

the school's newspaper and took four years of Latin and five of French. I was also a "hands-on" person who took four years of math and a year each of biology, chemistry, and physics, enjoying, in particular, the labs where we'd design and build experiments. In my senior year I won the school's prizes in French and Physics.

An English Major?

In 1954 I entered Princeton intending to major in Chemistry and pursue a dimly imagined, but definitely practical, career as a research chemist. But during the fourth semester of chemistry I changed my major to English. I made the change because I tired of the cookbook labs in qualitative and quantitative analysis. In quantitative analysis, in particular, I spent long hours in the balance room, calibrating the machine and weighing the precipitate I'd carefully collected and dried. The career I'd imagined, making better living through chemistry, suddenly seemed, in the spring afternoons I could see outside the lab, a horrible prospect. As luck and history would have it, I had taken just enough English courses to be able to complete an English major in the then-requisite four years.

Because of my late start and my science orientation, my undergraduate English major at Princeton was undistinguished, to say the least. As an undergraduate I never really understood what English was all about. Clearly it was "about" reading books—which I loved doing. But what else? In chemistry the questions were dull but nonetheless clear. What was this green substance in the test-tube? How much of this substance was there in the sample? At some later time we would inquire into the larger questions: the nature of matter itself. But in English, what questions were we trying to answer? What were these distinguished people —Louis Landa, Carlos Baker, Gerald Eades Bentley, Dudley Johnson—really up to? Where did it all lead, beyond personal pleasure?

During the summer of my sophomore year I found myself writing my first "junior paper," due in early fall, on Henry Fielding. I carefully read all of Fielding's novels and then sat down to write the requisite twenty pages—without any sense of where to begin. What did one say about these rather quaintly written books? What was there to say, except that one kept falling asleep while reading these books? My advisor asked me, after he had read the paper, why it was that I was majoring in English. I had, apparently, missed the boat.

I've realized since, as a result of my work in our writing-across-the-curriculum program, that I approached this English task, and others after it, in the spirit of the physical sciences. I could not write enough because I wanted to find that short, elegant single sentence that said what had to be said about Fielding's novels, or, later, the novels of Joseph Conrad. One of my roommates seemed to be able to write twenty pages on anything at all—a gift, I thought. I remember a seminar in Comparative Literature, one of those interminable two-hour, late-afternoon sessions in which one was to "discuss" a novel. We were reading, I think, Choderlos de Laclos' *Liaisons Dangereuses*. The seminar leader posed the question, one that was to carry us for two hours, she hoped: "What is the role of love in this novel?" There was general silence, and then, heart racing at 200 beats/second, I answered: "Without love, there would be no novel. Love drives the action." There was silence, and then embarrassed laughter. That was not an English answer. Later, in graduate school, trying to understand what I now know to be New Criticism, I asked, "What do we mean by *image*?" Same embarrassed laughter. Not an English question. I now know that it is encounters of this kind that define boundaries of social groups, or "discourse communities." At the time, however, the encounters produced their appropriate effect: I was taught that we simply didn't work this way in English. How we did work remained unclear to me.

Apprenticeship

After graduating in 1958 I went off to teach English at St. George's School, in Newport, Rhode Island, where I had been a student myself. At St. George's I found that I really loved teaching, and, surprising myself, that I loved teaching literature. Certainly there was anxiety. Would the students rise up and, in a body, leave the classroom? But there was also great satisfaction in helping students read and write. As I helped students make connections between their lives and particular works of literature I found myself making the connection myself, and I was surprised by the power I found in these works that had seemed just pleasant diversions. I thought until recently that I would have loved whatever I first did as a worker—that simply not being a student would have been enough. I believe now that I was amazingly fortunate at this particular moment. Not only were we between wars, in a time of relative peace when I really did not have to worry about the draft, but I had been invited to join the profession that validated my love of reading. Reading, as preparation for class, became "work" in my eyes and in the eyes of my family. My parents had stood by me when I changed my major from chemistry to English, but they were visibly pleased to see this "study" converted to "work" and the possibility of a career. Further, as a person born in 1936, I was entering a profession that, because it would serve the children of the post-World-War-II baby-boom, was in high demand.

At St. George's I taught, as one does in schools of this kind, eighth-grade World History, ninth- and tenth-grade English, five classes each day. I coached football (which I had loathed as a student), sailing, and swimming—which I could not do, but learned, in the pool, by myself, during free periods. Just twenty-one myself, I supervised a dormitory of eighteen-year-old post-adolescent males.

Most important in these years was my relationship with two other young teachers—George Carey and Geoff Spranger—both assigned, as I was, to teach tenth-grade English. We were entirely unsupervised—untrained and unwatched, and so we invented English for ourselves and for our students, drawing on our experience, which had been, entirely, the study of literature. Like so many in our profession, we'd never been taught writing. We'd exempted out of "bonehead English" and moved directly into the real stuff. We talked, often late into the night, never about our students' writing but about the literature we'd teach the next day. We brought to these discussions the energy peculiar to those who have to teach this same literature at 8:00 the next morning. I still have the textbook—Brown and Perrin's *A Quarto of Modern Literature*—on my shelves. I learned more about literature in these conversations than I had learned as an undergraduate and, perhaps, than I learned in graduate school where learning was, despite the seminar format, a distinctly private affair. The energy we three generated was enough to propel me through the Ph.D. George Carey went on to get his Ph.D. in folklore at Indiana and later came to the University of Massachusetts, where he now teaches folklore and writing—a fellow-maverick in a department of English. And Geoff Spranger went on to edit *Sail* magazine and to a career as a professional writer and editor.

On to the Ph.D.

Because teaching was not "work" enough—just daily delight, and because I could not imagine living out my life at St. George's School, and because I felt I needed to know more about literature if I were to continue to teach it—after two years at St. George's I headed off to Brown University for an MAT degree and a career in secondary-school English teaching. Once at Brown, I could not find the Education building, so I signed up for English courses—Shakespeare, The Modern Novel, and The Metaphysical Poets. With a career goal that gave me a reason for reading and writing about literature, I did so well in these courses that the Department chair, George Anderson, took me aside and told me that "I really should get my Ph.D. in English," and Barbara Lewalski invited me into her second-semester Milton seminar. I was being recruited—a nice feeling after my undergraduate experience with English. I learned later that the Department had inadvertently promised Milton seminars to Professors Lewalski and Millicent Bell in the same semester, and that both teachers were, therefore, trying to fill their seminars. The graduate program at Brown was small and would not normally support two concurrent Milton seminars. With my help, it did.

I moved through the Ph.D. program at Brown in what would now be considered good time—five years spent in graduate study, with a two-year teaching-break between the fourth and fifth years. But despite this progress, I never really felt comfortable in English. This discomfort surfaced in the comprehensive examinations, one of which I failed the first time through—not an uncommon experience in the program then, but a surprise to me and to the faculty, for I had done well in my course-work.

I trace my lack of comfort in the Brown graduate English program to the fact that I was not really suited to the Ph.D. in English as it was then conceived. I had developed a love for literature, as opposed to reading, late—through its teaching. Once in the classroom I had a practical reason for learning about literature—so that I could teach it better—and that furnished me with the motivation I needed to keep going. But what I was doing in the last years of graduate school had nothing to do with teaching. There was a part of me that did not believe in the intrinsic value of this entity called "literature" and of this activity called "literary criticism." In my work on Milton I'd been introduced to the world of biblical commentary, thousands of pages of commentary on the first

within it. Kay and her family helped me tremendously during this period—Kay coaching me as I memorized plots of Renaissance plays for the re-take of my comprehensive examination, and her parents quietly urging me on to complete the degree. Kay's father was a science teacher in the Washington, D.C., school system. Through NSF-funded summer institutes he had taught graduate-level courses to in-service teachers, but he had not himself been able to afford graduate study. Getting a Ph.D. thus meant a great deal to the Johnsons. When I did receive my degree I did not go to the commencement ceremony, which Kay's parents could not understand. Kay's mother bought me the Brown University Ph.D. hood for Christmas 1967.

In this last year at Brown, Edward Bloom, my thesis advisor, took me under his professional wing, helping me not only with the dissertation but with the job search. I have much to thank him for—and I remember a piece of advice he was moved to give me—good advice which I acted on for five years: "Charlie, you really should stay away from freshman writing programs. They have been the end of many a promising scholar."

In the Profession

With my new Ph.D. in hand I found work at the University of Massachusetts, a state university which was, in 1967, still expanding. In 1966, 1967, and 1968 the English Department hired twenty new Assistant Professors to teach the then-required two-semester sequence, "Masterpieces of Western Literature" and the hundreds of English majors this requirement produced. Following Edward Bloom's advice, I did not ask about Freshman Writing, nor was anything said to me about this course during the interview process. I remember now, though it did not seem remarkable at the time, that the Freshman Program was run by Arthur Williams, an embittered "terminal" Assistant Professor who thought so little of himself that when the Personnel Committee tried to promote him, he refused to be considered, saying that he was not qualified. There were other writing teachers in the Department—Marron DuBois, a fifty-ish Assistant Professor who taught writing to students in the vestigial Stockbridge School of Agriculture, combing their work for the error that she knew she'd find; Leonta Horrigan, also a perpetual Assistant Professor, a woman who had been a Dean in the old days but now, without a Ph.D., had been exiled to the teaching of writing; and Pamela Edwards, a bright part-time faculty spouse who was later put on the tenure track, given the University's Distinguished Teaching Award, and fired. Not only might the teaching of writing lead, as Bloom had said, to "the end of many a promising scholar." It seemed to lead to what I've learned to call "marginalization" and the bitterness and anger that accompanies this state.

The English Department I'd joined saw itself deeply committed to teaching: the teaching of literature. It was also, however, ambitious for its brand-new Ph.D. program and eager to achieve prestige through faculty publication. This situation—lots of young faculty and pressure to publish—could have become a shark-pit. And indeed I remember being told by a colleague that I should not talk out my ideas in the corridors because someone would steal them; and I remember watching another colleague so assiduously attach himself to senior colleagues that he'd not talk to us, his peers, all young fry who did not yet have the power to advance his career.

But this behavior was the exception. The Department's rapid expansion had shifted the balance of power in favor of the young and untenured. Most of us new faculty sided with a then-powerful liberal segment of the Department, one that had in 1961 founded *The Massachusetts Review*. This same group had just changed the Department's governing structure from one in which senior faculty held power to one in which power was distributed. All Departmental committees now had equal numbers of assistant, associate, and full professors. The young, untenured Assistant Professors felt, and were, powerful: we sat on all Departmental committees, including the Personnel Committee.

So when I heard from the chair and from other senior faculty that I'd have to begin publishing in my field right away if I wanted to stay, I listened, but to a mixed message. There were many tenured faculty in the Department who were not active scholars. In addition, because of the Department's representative governance, I knew that I'd have some say in the standards that were ultimately set for the award of tenure. And finally, given that the university was expanding and changing, emerging from a recent, land-grant "Mass Aggie" past, "English" was not a fixed entity. There might be room to move. Still, though I must have felt that I had an escape clause somewhere in my contract, I did see myself as a person who taught literature and who was an apprentice scholar in the field of literary studies. Everything I had learned as a Ph.D. candidate at Brown University, and most of what I had learned as a teacher in secondary schools, told me that English was the study of literature. And I swam, or dutifully tried to swim, in the mainstream.

In my first year at the university I taught literature—lots of it. In the fall semester I was assigned two sections of thirty-five students in the Masterpieces of Western Literature course, and one section of forty-two students in The Eighteenth Century Novel. The works in the "Master-pieces" course I'd read before only as means to some other end—*The Odyssey* as preparation for reading *Paradise Lost,* or *Oedipus* read to illuminate Shakespeare. So I read these works anew, or, in the case of Goeth's *Faust,* for the first time. Because so many of us were teaching the Masterpieces courses, we talked energetically about teaching, as I had at St. George's. I was learning new material still, and fast.

In my second semester I was asked to teach the Nineteenth Century British Novel—on the assumption, I suppose, that because I'd taught Fielding, Smollett, Sterne, and Richardson I could teach Thackeray, Trollope, Dickens, Charlotte Bronte, George Eliot, and Sir Walter Scott. I'd not read any of these novelists since eighth grade, but, unwilling to shake the English Department's confidence in me, I accepted the assignment and found myself reading the enormous novels and attendant criticism in preparation for the three hour-long weekly lectures I had to give. I can't imagine what I must have said or done in these courses. The "Dickens" and "George Eliot" materials I've purged long ago from my file cabinets, and the "Sterne" and "Fielding" materials also. These files—reading notes, thoughts for articles—have been entirely replaced by materials in composition theory. Whatever I did say and do in these undergraduate literature courses clearly had some force, for I have still in the files letters from students who thank me for teaching them so well and for inspiring them to go on to graduate study in English. I wonder now whether I won't be held accountable, in some future court, for what I have done.

Though on the surface I may have seemed a more-or-less conventional literature person, I was more than ready for a change of direction. I'd published a little, but there seemed no momentum in this publication. I'd followed an interest in the fiction of John Hawkes, who'd taught an exciting Modern Novel course at Brown, into two review-essays in *The Massachusetts Review,* and I'd written pieces on Trollope and Donald Barthelme that had grown out of my teaching. But I was walking down streets that were, for me, dead ends. Hawkes' fiction was moving further and further into mannered, self-reflexive prose. And I'd entirely lost interest in my dissertation subject, the fiction of Laurence Sterne. On my first sabbatical my family and I had travelled to Sterne's house and church, which I'd found unremarkable. Arthur Cash, a contemporary Sterne scholar, was raising funds to preserve Sterne's house. There seemed causes more deserving than this. Further, I'd taught an undergraduate seminar in Sterne and his literary forebears—Rabelais, Cervantes, Burton—and the undergraduates had helped me see that Sterne was not at all a pioneer, but was at best a great synthesizer and at worst simply derivative, far less interesting and valuable than his ancestors. In my eighteenth-century novel course I was teaching *Moll Flanders* and *Humphry Clinker*. Were these really great works of western literature?

The personnel files tell me that during this time I also threw myself into "service" activities that were teaching-related. I'd been, immediately on arrival, tapped for the department's Curriculum Committee, then Undergraduate Advisor, chair of our English Education committee, and Director of Undergraduate Studies. I'd helped redesign the English major, moving it in a direction that now looks quite modern: the study of writers, of genres, and of literary periods, in equal measure. No survey courses permitted. I conducted honors colloquia on modern fiction, and I was a "Faculty Fellow" in a campus dormitory, which meant bringing my family to dinner to meet my "corridor" and running a study group in the dormitory. The center of all this advising, committee work, and dormitory liaison was teaching—not literary study and scholarship, but teaching.

Moving On, or Coming Home

The impetus and opportunity I needed to propel me into the teaching of writing appeared in the person of Walker Gibson, who had come to the university in 1967 and gradually became important to me as model and as mentor. Here was a person who was committed to the teaching of writing who was, moreover, the most distinguished member of the Department. This was not a man on the margin; this was a "catch" for the university, a man who had published several volumes of poetry, a book on American prose style, and *Persona*, an influential and humane writing textbook. The English Department had senior literary scholars who would gladly have accepted my apprenticeship had I sought them out. That I had not asked for their help is yet another sign that at a deep level I did not want to follow their lead. But Walker Gibson was someone I wanted to know. A bright and irreverent man, his style was a welcome relief from the to-me-groundless seriousness of some of our literary scholars and MFA writers. Gibson had come to the university to re-make the moribund freshman writing course. Seeing that the English Department really did not want freshman English, in 1970 Gibson took the program out of the department, making it an autonomous Rhetoric Program that reported directly to the Provost's Office. This move was seen by the Department as entirely positive; now we would not have to think about freshman writing. As Gerald Graff has noted, English Departments in America react to a call for change by hiring one person in the new area and then continuing on as before. Now that we had our person in Rhetoric, we could press on to important matters.

Gibson was both the most distinguished person in our Department and an outsider. Despite his solid credentials in English, he was not accepted by the people at the center of the department, nor did he court such acceptance. He might have remained so had not the university in 1969 brought in a new department head, Joe Frank, a Milton scholar who was given to asking the question, "Could any of us prove that Milton was a better writer than James Baldwin?" This, in 1969, was heady stuff. Frank's arrival coincided with a radical change in the academic environment, one that was not at all favorable to English. In the political heat of 1969–70 the university had dropped its Masterpieces of Western Literature requirement, which had supplied the English Department with thousands of guaranteed students and had fuelled the Department's expansion. In the same year, the Department had abandoned the two-semester freshman writing sequence and its guaranteed supply of students. By 1971 we were therefore a department of 107 with a scandalously low enrollment, an obvious target for retrenchment. Seeing this situation beginning to develop, the department sought enrollment wherever it might be found.

In this new context Walker Gibson was, in Joe Frank's eyes, potentially the Department's salvation. Gibson established contacts in our School of Education and through these contacts engaged a number of us in projects that the university then termed "Outreach." In Spring 1971 I signed on for the Career Opportunities Program, which involved flying in a tiny plane from nearby Northampton to Flushing Airport in Queens, then taking a taxi to a building in the Bedford-Stuyvesant section of

New York City, then, still slightly air- and car-sick, teaching literature and writing to middle-aged teacher's aides, mostly black and female, then jumping back into the cab, and the plane, and flying back to Northampton—all in the space of eight hours.

This was "real" work, valuable in a way that teaching Smollett and Richardson, or even Fielding and Johnson, was not. The teachers' aides were in a degree-program that would bring them certification and the promise of full-time teaching positions in the city's school system. Never mind that the program was mismanaged; never mind that it was located not in New York City but in Amherst. This was adventure, this was teaching, and it felt useful. Gibson and Frank also made a connection with the local jail and we were invited in to teach English. Here we taught literature writing—in really awful surroundings, often to students sedated beyond the possibility of learning. We tried to teach subjects, but what was really possible in this context was working with the inmates' own writing. I developed strong personal relationships with a number of the inmates—mostly black, mostly in jail because they had not been very good at their work: stealing cars, armed robbery—not drugs, yet.

Through Joe Frank and Walker Gibson we also made contact with Mina Shaughnessy and her work at CCNY. Joe Frank asked me if I'd agree to work in her lab and bring graduate students with me, as training for them and for us. So it came to pass that in fall of 1972 three of us drove every Thursday from Amherst to New York City, leaving at 4:30 in the morning, arriving at the CCNY Instructional Resource Center at 8:00 A.M., tutoring there until noon, and then returning to Amherst. We met and talked with Shaughnessy and her staff, collected materials and strategies, and reported back to the department. The spirit of Shaughnessy's operation made a deep impression on all of us. The materials did not. In the actual tutoring in the lab, the elaborate system of numbered grammar-based worksheets proved not usable. But the larger aim, to help a new population of students achieve the literacy they needed, was exciting and seemed to us then, as it does now, an important part of "English."

In this same year Jim Leheny, a colleague, also an eighteenth-century scholar and a companion on long weekend runs through the woods, was making contact with the Springfield, Massachusetts, school system. Springfield presented the possibility of an urban teaching experience for our entirely suburban MAT program. Would I come along and co-teach this MAT seminar? The project had both Frank's and Gibson's blessing and, with my tenure decision now in the hands of the Dean's Personnel Committee, I signed on. Leheny had met Roger Garrison at a teacher-training workshop and brought back an enthusiastic report and a copy of Garrison's underground monograph, "An Approach to Tutorial Instruction in Freshman Composition." I read these materials, mimeographed and unpretentious, and they seemed honest and true. Who could, after reading this, imagine again standing before a class of twenty students and talking about writing? Garrison spoke of the writing teacher as editor and coach. At this same time I had been given a copy of Donald Murray's *A Writer Teaches Writing* by one of our MFA graduate students, and I read this too. Here it was again—two men, both New Englanders, both journalists by training, each entirely unaware of the other's work, saying the same smart things.

What Garrison and Murray said resonated with what I'd experienced in my teaching. In fall 1972, in the same semester that I worked in Mina Shaughnessy's CCNY lab, I taught my first on-campus writing course at the university. The English Department's need for enrollment had driven us to this: we opened up our Advanced Expository Writing course and invited the university in. I met my first class of twenty students, realized after one class meeting that I could not teach this as a stand-up, talk-about-writing course, and turned the class into a system of one-to-one tutorials, meeting each student for thirty minutes once each week. This was a desperate move, not planned, but taken because the class as I'd begun to teach it—talking about writing—was so dreadful. What could one say to a group that included an engineer, a flower-child, a native speaker of Chinese who had been in America for two years, an exchange student from the University of London? Given my sympathy with Murray's and Garrison's work, I did not see that the students might have quite a bit to say to one another. Had I done so, the class would have taken a rather different turn, toward group-work and peer responding. What I did see was that if I were to be the students' writing coach, I'd have to work with them individually.

The tutorials were tremendous fun. They were work too; if I taught two sections of twenty students in this manner, I spent twenty to twenty-five hours a week in my office, with a schedule like a dentist's, seeing a new student every thirty minutes. But in these tutorials I could see, for the first time in my teaching career, the actual results of my teaching. If I said to a student, "I think you ought to throw more light here and here, re-write, and bring it in next week," in a week the results of that advice would be there, on my desk. If I liked the results, fine; if not, fine too—I'd learned something about how this particular writer, in this particular writing situation, responded to a specific editorial intervention. Here was a lab, ready made, for the study of writing pedagogy. No more guessing at the effects of my teaching. Here were the results, inescapable.

I taught writing in this way for the next four years, learning as I went, and so enthusiastic about what I was doing that many in the department, also drafted into the teaching of expository writing, followed suit. In 1976 we offered thirty-six faculty-taught sections of Advanced Expository Writing. Fourteen of these sections were taught by tutorial. In 1976 Joe Skerrett and I gave a paper at CCCC on what we were seeing in these tutorials. While browsing in the CCCC book display I found Janet Emig's monograph *The Composing Processes of Twelfth Graders,* more support for the direction I was taking.

This teaching experience, and my delight in it, led to what my personnel files tell me is a surge of professional activity. From 1967–79 my Annual Reports—summaries of what I had done in a given year—are quick reading. In these years I turned in this report at the last possible moment, hoping, as I do with my taxes, that late returns are less likely to be audited. But beginning in fall 1979 the forms are filled with actual and imminent publication in journals such as *College English, College Composition and Communication,* and *The Journal of English Teaching Techniques,* with the record of papers given at conferences, and with the record of teacher-training workshops given in schools and writing workshops at business sites. Now, in 1979 I began to assemble my Annual Report with care and turn it in well before the deadline. In this same year I taught the last literature course I'd teach, one that became the basis for an article, "Teaching Writing/Teaching Literature" that was accepted by Richard Larson for *CCC.* I was now a writing teacher. I was going to conferences, I was reading journals, I was publishing articles in these same journals. I was, it seemed, at last at home in my profession.

The teaching-by-tutorial, coupled with our work with the Springfield Schools, led to two NEH-funded Institutes for the Teaching of Writing which I directed in 1978–79 and 1980–81. The institutes, again Walker Gibson's idea, brought me deeper into the world of writing and its teaching. Walker saw that we were beginning to develop a writing group in the Department, so he brought four of us together—Jim Leheny, Joe Skerrett, C. K. Smith and myself. He suggested that we apply for an "Extended Teacher Institute" grant and guided us through the application process. And so it came to pass that NEH sent us a huge check and that in the summer of 1978 fifty secondary English teachers spent six weeks with us learning about writing and its teaching. Leheny and I came at our subject from a perspective deeply influenced by Murray, Garrison, and Emig. Because we considered the teachers to be writers, we built a great deal of teacher-writing into the program. In addition, we traveled with our teachers into Springfield, where we tutored summer-school writing students, kept records of our editorial interventions, and in a post-tutorial seminar reflected on what we'd done in the light of the results we'd achieved. Joe Skerrett, who had read and been influenced by the work of James Moffett, believed that writing arose out of talk, and so his part of the Institute was deeply dialogic. C. K. Smith, a polymath and neo-Aristotelian, believed that a writer's chief difficulty was generating material, and so his part of the program engaged the teachers in "thinking" exercises— "heuristics," as I've learned to call them. Through Skerrett and Smith I discovered the limits of the Murray-Garrison, craft-based model I'd started with. There was a lot to read and know, apparently, in this field.

The NEH Institutes led to a decade of work in Massachusetts high schools through what came to be known as the UMass/Amherst Writing Project. In the course of this off-campus teaching we created a network of writing teachers that is still active. We established "demonstration sites" at schools with exemplary writing programs, and we encouraged Massachusetts teachers to visit these sites. I talked often with Jim Gray about affiliating with the National Writing Network, but both of us agreed that there was no pressing advantage to this affiliation. So we continued on, funded by various aspects of the state, until funding for writing projects dried up absolutely in 1987. In that year, in recognition of this work in Massachusetts secondary schools, the Massachusetts Council of Teachers of English gave me its F. Andre Favat award for "Distinguished Contributions to the English Language Arts."

The Institutes led to my acquaintance with hundreds of dedicated English teachers, some now among my most valued friends and colleagues. The Institutes also brought me into contact with some of the most productive and luminous people in our field. I'd met Don Murray in 1977, through students we'd both taught, and through Walker Gibson

I'd met others—Gary Tate, Richard Lloyd-Jones, Lynn Troyka, Ed Corbett—at CCCC conventions. To our 1979 Institute we invited Lee Odell and Nancy Martin, and to our 1981 Institute we invited Peter Elbow and Anne Herrington. Six years later Elbow and Herrington would come to the University as colleagues. I'm still in touch with Nancy Martin, principally as the author of an essay that will be for a book on writing in the disciplines that Herrington and I have prepared for MLA. But the meeting with Lee Odell led to the quickest result: a phone call from SUNY-Albany asking me to teach their Composition Theory course in Fall 1981. Odell had left SUNY-Albany to go to Rensselaer Polytechnic Institute, and Eugene Garber was looking for a substitute. Along with the course came a lecture-budget with which I was to bring in the best people then in the field. So invitations went out to Linda Flower, Nancy Sommers, Peter Elbow, and Elaine Maimon. Garber set this all up beautifully, making sure that I was able to meet and talk with the visitors and integrate their presentations with the course I was giving. I could not have dreamed a better introduction to my new field.

In 1981, which now seems an "annus mirabilis" for me, I also helped set in motion a sequence of events that would lead to the establishment of the University Writing Program, which I directed from 1982 through Spring 1989. In retrospect, this was for me the perfect opportunity: a combination of teacher-training, which I'd been prepared for by the Institutes, graduate teaching in composition studies, which I had been engaged in since 1977, the teaching of writing, which I'd been doing since 1972, and the administrative skills that I'd learned both as Director of the NEH Institutes and from my two-year stint as Acting Chair of the English Department.

That this opportunity came my way was no accident. In 1981–82 the English Department was still suffering from the low enrollments that had been its fate since it had lost both the Masterpieces courses and Freshman English. As a result, the department had been reduced in size, through attrition and denial of tenure, from 107 in 1971 to 78 in 1982. The Rhetoric Program, with its guaranteed freshman enrollment and its TA budget, began to look like a way out of the departmental decline. In addition, the Dean of our unit was squeezing the Rhetoric Program's budget, making it difficult for the unit to function. Rumors that the program was doomed began to circulate within the university community. As the rumors took hold, students began to postpone taking their required courses and a backlog of un-taught students began to accumulate, a situation that was, from the Provost's perspective, an administrative nightmare.

In Fall 1981 the Provost therefore called for a Rhetoric Study Committee, chaired by Jim Leheny, of the Springfield connection. In addition the Provost asked Leheny, Joe Skerrett, and me to design a Writing Program that would suit our institution. I did a quick draft, sketching out a three-credit freshman requirement that would be a "studio" writing course and a junior-year writing program that would be given by academic departments for their majors. This design was the outcome of two recent experiences I'd had: the SUNY-Albany graduate teaching, where I had assigned Elaine Maimon's *Writing in the Arts and Sciences* and had heard her speak, with her usual passion and conviction; and our 1981 NEH Institute, where I'd met and talked with Nancy Martin. The Rhetoric Study Committee took my draft, put it together with materials they had solicited from the University of Michigan and elsewhere, and produced a report recommending that the university disband the Rhetoric Program and create a University Writing Program along the lines I'd suggested. The Committee recommended that the program be housed in English, but that it have a separate budget, one clearly defined and understood to belong to the Program. The Committee also recommended that the Director be a member of the English Department but that the Writing Program as a whole be responsible to a University Writing Committee which was to be composed of faculty from across the disciplines. This design has kept the Writing Program moderately secure and insulated it from the forces that have brought the Rhetoric Program, and programs like it at other institutions, to their knees.

So in Spring 1982, the University Writing Program became law, and I its executive officer. Though I have been the administrator of this program, which is no small task—the program includes a support staff of five, a teaching staff of some seventy-five to eighty-five teaching assistants, and has taught 4,400 students a year—I have not considered myself an administrator. Administration in the service of the teaching of writing seems useful, but academic administration in general is, for me, too far removed from teaching.

The new Writing Program has brought me two great personal benefits. The first is that through the program, and through its department-based junior-year writing component, I have come to know faculty across the university who are interested in undergraduate teaching. The junior-year writing program has become an informal, faculty-development-program-without-portfolio, one of the places where we talk directly about undergraduate teaching. Through Bill Mullin, the professor of Physics who directs the junior-year program, I have learned about writing in the physical sciences, and through Sylvia Forman, the chair of our Anthropology Department who also teaches that department's writing course, I have come to know something about writing in the social sciences. As a result of this learning and teaching I feel now more like a university citizen than a member of a particular department.

The second personal benefit is that the Writing Program has become the occasion for hiring colleagues whose professional interests coincide with mine. My co-conspirators in the NEH Institutes and in the early stages of the Writing Program have all moved in other directions: Joe Skerrett into scholarship in American Studies and Jim Leheny into full-time administration. In their place, and in place of Walker Gibson, who has retired, we have brought on board Anne Herrington and Peter Elbow. With three of us here we now have the critical mass to support a small graduate program in Rhetoric and Composition. We three meet for lunch on Wednesdays, talk over our projects and our shared work, and bring news from our respective fields of interest. We look forward to bringing a fourth person here to strengthen both the Writing Program and our new graduate program.

Where to from here? As I write this, I am about to turn the Writing Program over to Anne Herrington. It seems the right time to do this. I know the program must evolve, yet I don't want to manage the change—a clear sign that I should step down. And further, with Anne and Peter now colleagues, I don't feel the need to lead. We have become a collective of sorts, sharing drafts of articles and ideas and working together in determining policy for the program. Anne will run the program, but I'll still teach, still work with TAs, and still teach in our new graduate program. I do not see myself "coming back," as some of my colleagues put it, to the teaching of literature. I've left that behind me. I have too much to learn in my new field. During a sabbatical semester I read Aristotle and Plato with a Communications seminar, but I still have a long way to go before I feel easy in the world of Rhetoric. Further, with Anne Herrington's encouragement I've begun a qualitative research project in our computer labs. And Anne has asked me to co-edit with her a book on writing in the disciplines. In addition, I want to pursue my interest in the ways in which developments in computer technology may be altering the act of writing itself. To the extent this is so, we'll have to develop new ways of teaching writing. For now, the projects multiply, and time becomes more precious. Only ten more years before retirement!

I said at the outset that I wanted to find out why I am what I am: a Professor of English, trained as a specialist in literary scholarship, who left the world of literary studies in the 1970s and entered the field of composition studies. I'd like to think that I have come to some answers, insofar as it is possible to know oneself. And the answers I've come to are very much like those I saw on the horizon when I set out on this voyage of discovery.

I've looked first into my own history, finding there the origin of a somewhat unconventional English person, someone who might, with different luck, have become a scientist. I'm a reader and a writer, but someone who needs to connect that reading and writing with an immediate and practical present. Teaching is a way I've found of making reading and writing an applied discipline. My classroom is my laboratory. As a faculty member in an English department at a major research university, I've found that my interest in teaching has drawn me toward composition studies, a place in English where we do talk about teaching. In composition studies we do not have literature as a potential "subject" to study and talk about. There is, I'd argue, despite the proliferation of our journals, no "subject" in our field; there is activity, and talk and writing about that activity. And this suits me just fine.

I've been able to move into composition studies in part because of circumstance—what I consider good fortune. I was born in 1936, white and male, part of an extremely small cohort, one that was called on to teach the much larger cohorts of the baby boom of 1946–60. When I received my Ph.D. in English I found myself in demand. In addition, as a man and head-of-household in the 1960s, I had behind me the impetus of family expectations and support. With these powerful engines available to me I was able to push on through examinations, dissertations, and the uncertainties of the job-search—any one of which could have stopped me dead in the water. Moreover, when I began to teach at the university, the expansion of American post-secondary education in the late 1960s and early 1970s shook the system considerably, and English with it. In this fluid situation I was able to evolve as I had to and to move into the teaching of writing.

My existence in "English" is now secure, given tenure and seniority, but I still feel that old discomfort. Somehow I do not quite belong. I accept part of the responsibility for this discomfort. It may be that I'd not absolutely fit anywhere. But I also feel that English is itself pursuing a bit of a dead end and that my discomfort is likely shared by many of us—even those of us who continue to work in literary studies. Unlike physics or chemistry or engineering, English is ineluctably tied to teaching. Yet we've tried to emulate the "hard" sciences by creating a category of activity in our field that we call "research" and, in institutions where this research is valued—the high-prestige and high-salary institutions—steadily decreasing the amount of teaching we do. It seems to me that our recent attraction to post-structuralist theory is a further move in the same direction. But the present shape of English is not inevitable or true. What would English be like today had we followed Louise Rosenblatt's lead, and not that of Wimsatt, Brooks, and Warren, in the 1930s?

It may be that in composition studies we are really OK and that it is our colleagues in literary studies who are the epicycle. There are signs that this may indeed be the case. The field of composition studies is prospering. Our graduate students find themselves in high demand, and we find ourselves in demand as well, able to move if we should choose to do so. It may be that events will force a redefinition of English. If so, we'll be there to participate. I am, therefore, looking forward to the next decade in composition studies. There's work to be done and fine people to work with. This is altogether a good life, this life I live in our profession.

Index

AAUP. *See* American Association of University Professors
ABC program, 168
Abstracts, 89
Academic staff position, vs. tenure status, 144
Accreditation, 150
American Association of University Professors (AAUP), 149–50
American Educational Research Association, 99
"Analogical-theoretical research," 55
Analysis, in network of symbolic action, 26–27
Aristotelian tradition, meaning of rhetoric in, 19–20
Aristotle, 41
Arts and Humanities Citation Index, 90
Audience relatedness, 85

Bain, Alexander, 63, 64
Bedford Bibliography for Teachers of Writing (Gorrell, Bizzell, and Herzberg, eds.), 75–76, 80
Bibliographical control problem, 81–82
Bibliographical resources. *See also* Source materials
character of, 75
composition history and, 61–62
evaluation problem in, 77–78
functions in composition bibliography and, 85–86
for research in historical rhetoric, 79–80
for research on composition, 75–79
review-essay pattern in, 73–75
search strategies and, 86–90
serial bibliography and, 80–84

subject classification and, 83–84, 86, 89–90
Biography, 60
Blair, Hugh, 41
Boundaries, challenges to, 9–10
Brown University, 166–68, 169
Burke, Kenneth, 41

Campbell, George, 41
Case study research, 106–7
CCCC. *See* Conference on College Composition and Communication
CCCC Bibliography of Composition and Rhetoric (Lindemann, ed.), 61, 82–84, 89, 91n5
CCC. See *College Composition and Communication*
Choate School, 168
Cicero, 41
Citation indexes, 89–90
City College of New York (CCNY), 174, 175
Classical sources, 16–17, 26
Cognitive processes, 96–97
College Composition and Communication (CCC), 40, 53, 122
Larson's bibliography in, 74, 81, 83
College English (journal), 40, 52
Composing processes, 96. *See also* Teaching of writing
Composition
meanings of term, 15–18, 30, 85
psychology of, 96
Composition as a Human Science: Contributions to the Self-Understanding of a Discipline (Phelps), 17, 96, 97, 130

183